POLICY COMPETITION AND FOREIGN DIRECT INVESTMENT IN EUROPE

Other titles in the collection

EU Enlargement
Cohesion and regional policy
Edited by John Bachtler, Ruth Downes and Grzegorz Gorzelak

Policy Competition and Foreign Direct Investment in Europe

Edited by
PHILIP RAINES and ROSS BROWN
European Policies Research Centre
University of Strathclyde
Glasgow

Ashgate

Aldershot • Brookfield USA • Singapore • Sydney

Published by
Ashgate Publishing Ltd
Gower House
Croft Road
Aldershot
Hants GU11 3HR
England

Ashgate Publishing Company
Old Post Road
Brookfield
Vermont 05036
USA

British Library Cataloguing in Publication Data
Policy competition and foreign direct investment in Europe
 1. Investments, Foreign - Europe 2. Investments, Foreign -
 Government policy - Europe 3. Competition - Europe
 I. Raines, Philip II. Brown, Ross
 332.6'73'094

Library of Congress Catalog Card Number: 98-74932

ISBN 1 84014 768 7

Printed and bound by Athenaeum Press, Ltd.,
Gateshead, Tyne & Wear.

Contents

Preface

The OECD Development Centre has undertaken a wide-ranging programme of research to understand the relationship between government policy and global foreign investment flows. As part of this programme, it has commissioned a series of studies investigating the activities of governments in different global regions in attracting investment and how competition between governments has shaped the design and implementation of policy. A synthesis of the findings of the programme will appear in Charles Oman (forthcoming 1999) *Policy Competition and Foreign Direct Investment* (OECD Development Centre, Paris). Based on a review of existing research literature and statistical sources, the following report was produced on policy competition and the attraction of foreign investment in Europe. The information presented was current at the time of the study's production, that is, January 1998. The study was prepared by staff at the European Policies Research Centre based at the University of Strathclyde under the direction of Professor John Bachtler:

- Dr Ross Brown (Research Fellow)
- Dr Keith Clement (Associate Fellow)
- Ewa Helinska-Hughes (Research Fellow)
- Philip Raines (Senior Research Fellow)
- Fiona Wishlade (Senior Research Fellow)

The chapter on FDI policy in Central and Eastern Europe was written in collaboration with Professor Michael Hughes of the University of Stirling.

Philip Raines
Ross Brown
EPRC
Glasgow

Acknowledgements

The editors wish to acknowledge the advice and support of Charles Oman of the OECD Development Centre in the structure and content of the study, and Moira Lowe of EPRC for her patience in formatting the book for publication.

In addition, the following organisations are acknowledged for granting permission to use and reproduce copyright material.

In Chapter 2, Table 2.1: ©United Nations, 1997. Table extracted from *World Investment Report 1997* by kind permission of the Publishers, the United Nations.

In Chapter 2, Table 2.2: ©European Communities, 1993. Table extracted from *Regional Development – New Location Factors for Mobile Investment in Europe* by kind permission of the Publishers, the Office for Official Publications of the European Communities.

In Chapter 6, Table 6.2: ©OECD, 1991. Table extracted from *Taxing Profits in a Global Economy: Domestic and International Issues* by kind permission of the OECD.

In Chapter 6, quote: ©OECD, 1996. Quote taken from *Tax Expenditures: Recent Experiences* by kind permission of the OECD.

1   Introduction

PHILIP RAINES AND ROSS BROWN

Foreign direct investment (FDI) has expanded rapidly throughout the world economy over the last two decades. This trend has been promoted by the removal of national barriers to capital movements and increasing globalisation, especially by multinational enterprises (MNEs). The aggregate stock of FDI in the world economy is estimated to have risen from 4.5 percent of world output in 1975 to 9.5 percent in 1994, with the value of sales by foreign affiliates of domestic companies exceeding the value of world exports by around a quarter (Barrel and Pain, 1997). Between 1980 and 1989, accumulated FDI inflows among developed countries were more than four times as large as during the 1970s, with FDI growing faster in the 1980s than GDP and trade by factors of four and three respectively (Neven and Siotis, 1993).

Widespread attention has been given to charting how the global rise in these investment flows has been associated with changes in the operation and inter-relationships of national and regional economies - such as the globalisation of production and increasing international economic interdependency. Less research has been carried out on the impact of rising FDI on government policy, not just on the overall objectives of economic policy, but the types of micro-economic and regulatory policies favoured by governments.

The policy impact is evident at different levels. International responses to FDI growth have included efforts to establish collective frameworks on the treatment of foreign investors, notably the OECD's Multilateral Agreement on Investment and the agreement brokered through the World Trade Organisation on trade-related investment measures (TRIMs). At national level, recognition of the role of foreign investment in regenerating local economies and creating employment has resulted in policies being specially devised for attracting and retaining FDI, involving the coordination of existing policy instruments, the creation of new ones, the allocation of increasing resources to FDI policies and the development of institutional structures for delivering different elements of these policies. The work of national governments has been mirrored by similar approaches taken sub-nationally, as regional governments and local authorities and agencies have pursued their own individual policies in competing for FDI.

In Europe, this process of FDI policy development at different levels has perhaps advanced further than elsewhere in the world. The importance of attracting foreign investment has been acknowledged by local and national governments as well as by larger groups such as the European Union. At the same time, the need to set competition within limits has also been recognised, leading to the emergence of detailed controls on industrial subsidies and incentives at European level by the European Commission. Although the nature of this competition is changing with the continent's realignment in response to the liberalisation and restructuring of the economies of Central and Eastern Europe (CEE), policy competition remains the driving force behind the scale and type of approaches to regulating and attracting foreign investment.

The following study addresses the issue of policy competition in Europe by considering three sets of questions. First, it will gauge the level of policy competition in Europe, assessing the extent to which governments in both Western and CEE governments have positive attitudes towards encouraging foreign investment and detailing the main policy areas and approaches used by governments. Second, the question of whether policy competition is increasing will be answered as the study identifies the different factors influencing future changes in FDI trends and likely policy responses to these changes. Lastly, the study will examine the effects of policy competition in Europe: has inter-governmental rivalry encouraged an overall rise in FDI, increased investment in human capital and infrastructure, more open national markets and a more secure legal environment, or has it led to costly 'bidding wars' between countries, involving rising incentive budgets and diminishing labour and environmental standards?   More importantly, where competition has produced harmful effects, have systems been put in place to limit the damage caused and control the rivalry?

In addition to this introduction and the conclusions, the study is divided into two sections. The first section sets the *policy context* for foreign investment competition in Europe in two chapters. The first chapter focuses on Western Europe: recent trends in foreign investment flows, the different approaches of national and European Community policy-makers to foreign ownership of the economy, and the institutional structures that exist to promote foreign investment. Given the substantial differences between FDI trends and policy issues in Western European and CEE countries, FDI policy in CEE is reviewed separately in Chapter 2 (though aspects of it are considered in some of the later chapters, as appropriate).

The second section of the study examines *policy competition* in specific policy areas, principally in Western Europe. A wide range of policies influences FDI flows, often in areas not directly linked to FDI - eg. local content regulations in trade policy will affect whether external companies locate within a trade area, and macroeconomic policy will determine whether national markets are sufficiently attractive and stable for potential foreign investors. This study focuses only on policies that have been explicitly linked to the regulation and attraction of foreign investment in Europe. Although the policy areas vary in terms of the degree to which FDI considerations have shaped their development - and consequently, the extent to which they can be described as 'FDI policies' - they have all had a visible FDI dimension in Europe over the past decade.

The policies can be divided into those which are 'incentive-based', aiming to influence location decisions directly by subsidising the establishment (and to some extent, operating) costs of investment locations - such as regional financial aids and tax incentives - and those which are 'rule-based', which have a more indirect impact on costs by affecting the regulatory and operating environments of foreign investors - such as labour and environmental standards, and controls on the use of financial incentives.

Three final points require clarification. First, for the purposes of this discussion, FDI is defined as 'an investment involving a long-term relationship and reflecting a lasting interest and control of a resident entity in one economy (foreign direct investor or parent enterprise) in an enterprise resident in an economy other than that of the foreign direct investor (FDI enterprise or affiliate enterprise or foreign affiliate)' (UNCTAD, 1996). With the focus on the more direct and longer-term impacts of investment, portfolio investment flows and the policies affecting those flows have not been considered here.

Second, the study will make reference to rules and policies in the 'European Union' and the 'European Community' interchangeably. This reflects the fact that, since the signature of the Maastricht Treaty, the term

'European Union' has entered into common parlance to refer to actions conducted at the European level. Technically, however, European competition, employment and environmental policies remain *European Community* (EC) policies. These remained substantially unchanged under the recent Treaty of European Union which added two 'pillars' of inter-governmental cooperation and coordination (Justice and Home Affairs and Common Foreign and Security) to the existing EC provisions.

Lastly, the study was finalised by the end of 1997 and consequently, does not discuss in detail more recent developments in certain areas, notably the introduction of proposed codes on tax incentives and the use of financial incentives for large foreign investment projects in the EU.

Part I:
Policy Context

2 FDI Policy Approaches in Western Europe

ROSS BROWN AND PHILIP RAINES

Introduction

In over two decades of active FDI promotion, Western European approaches to attracting foreign investment have been characterised by increasing activity and sophistication in both policy design and delivery. While largely responding to the impact of greater competition between governments at a time of larger FDI flows, the scale and variety of policy responses reflect a realisation that investment promotion requires both the designation of clear administrative responsibilities within government and a more adept use of both incentive- and rule-based approaches to attracting FDI. Hence, at the same time as European countries have defined comprehensive national policies on foreign investment, they have developed institutional mechanisms for delivering different aspects of FDI policy. Hardly anywhere in Western Europe currently regards the attraction of FDI projects as an *ad hoc* policy activity: virtually every European country has considered FDI sufficiently important to warrant a set of specific policies and organisations (although with widely varying degrees of priority).

In this chapter, the policy *context* for the whole of Western Europe is considered, providing a background for understanding the scale and effects of policy competition. Following this introduction, the *statistical* context of FDI policy is reviewed in the second and third sections, through a summary of the main investment trends in Western Europe in recent years and the current and likely future factors determining these flows. The fourth and fifth sections focus on the *strategic* context of policy by examining the importance of foreign investment as a goal for Western

European governments, both from the perspective of the differing national as well as European Community approaches to the regulation of foreign ownership in the economy. Finally, the *institutional* context is analysed with respect to the organisations promoting foreign investment and the approaches developed by inward investment organisations at national and local levels.

Foreign Investment in Western Europe

The United States remains the country receiving the largest inward investment flow - US$ 85 billion in 1996 (UNCTAD, 1997). As a region though, Western Europe is currently the main destination for worldwide FDI. Inward flows were US$ 105 billion in 1996, accounting for about a third of global inward investment. Its share of the global stock of FDI has been increasing over the past decade, rising from 33 percent in 1985, peaking at 44 percent in 1990 before falling back to 40 percent in 1996.

Several distinct geographical features characterise current FDI flows in Western Europe. Although short-term FDI inflows fluctuate quite substantially, the spatial distribution of FDI seems quite fixed over the long term and these patterns appear to be part of longer term trends where certain countries and regions dominate Western Europe's FDI inflows.

Three countries - the United Kingdom, Germany and France - account for over half of the stock of FDI in Western Europe and annual average inflows during the 1980s and 1990s (Table 2.1). The Western European country which has undoubtedly been most attractive to incoming FDI is the *UK*. The historical pattern of Europe's FDI flows shows that the UK is consistently the most important investment location, both in terms of stocks as well as recent inflows. This has been particularly true in terms of non-European FDI, as the UK has attracted 40 percent of US FDI in Europe and more than 40 percent of FDI from Japan and Asia's tiger economies. In global terms, the UK continues to be the world's second largest recipient of inward investment after the US (UNCTAD, 1997). Reflecting the openness of the economy, sales of British businesses to overseas investors were estimated to have exceeded the total for all other EU countries combined during 1996 (IBB, 1997).

Table 2.1 FDI in Western Europe

	(US$ millions)				FDI as % of GDP	
Host region/ economy	*1984-9 (annual average)*	*1990-5 (annual average)*	*1996 Inward flows*	*1996 Inward stock*	*1980*	*1994*
Austria	318	837	3,806	19,886	5.8	6.6
Belg/Lux	2,793	9,336	13,920	100,767	6.0	31.7
Denmark	323	2,297	773	23,393	6.3	12.6
Finland	314	1,205	1,227	9,401	1.1	5.9
France	5,364	18,031	20,809	168,432	3.4	10.7
Germany	1,833	2,568	3,851	170,989	4.5	6.8
Greece	624	1,022	1,004	20,310	11.3	23.5
Ireland	85	95	1,455	13,953	19.5	10.3
Italy	2,560	3,702	3,739	74,991	2.0	5.9
Neths.	3,787	7,844	6,290	118,626	11.3	27.7
Portugal	639	1,848	607	6,747	4.4	6.6
Spain	4,535	10,918	6,396	104,976	2.4	25.0
Sweden	982	5,343	5,484	42,007	2.9	9.7
UK	13,545	19,674	30,053	344,703	11.7	20.9
Other W. Europe	2,052	3,054	5,963	83,306	n.a.	n.a.
All W. Europe	39,754	87,774	105,377	1,302,487	5.7	13.0

Source: UNCTAD (1997).

Inward investment is largely concentrated in the northern, more developed countries in Western Europe. In recent years, one of the most important locations for FDI has been *France*, which had FDI inflows totalling US$ 20.8 billion in 1996, a figure which places France second in Western Europe's league of FDI. Indeed, in terms of flows, France briefly overtook the UK as Europe's top destination for incoming FDI in 1994.

Not surprisingly, *Germany* is another major destination for FDI, though its importance appears to have diminished in recent years. Although Germany has the second largest FDI stocks in Western Europe, its inward flows seem to have declined sharply in recent years, so that in spite of being the largest economy in the region, it only received 3.7 percent of FDI flows in 1996, leaving the country with one of the lowest FDI-to-GDP ratios (Table 2.1). Moreover, these inflows have been dwarfed by the massive FDI outflows of US$ 28.6 billion (UNCTAD, 1997). Germany's imbalance between outflows and inflows reached US$ 24.8 billion in 1996. While some commentators note that the difference may have been exaggerated by distortions arising from Bundesbank data-gathering (Döhrn, 1996), fears have been regularly cited of a potential 'hollowing out' process in German industry (see, for example, Tüselmann, 1995).

Interestingly, some of Europe's smaller economies are also major recipients of incoming FDI, particularly *Belgium-Luxembourg* and the *Netherlands*. In fact even during the early 1990s when Europe's FDI flows were subdued, some smaller European countries experienced increasing FDI flows (eg. Belgium-Luxembourg). Average flows for Belgium-Luxembourg between 1990-95 were over treble what they had been between 1984-89 (Table 2.1). The Netherlands has the fourth largest stock of foreign investment in Western Europe, accounting for nine percent of the total stock. FDI as a share of GDP is also high in these small, centrally-located countries. Foreign investment in Belgium-Luxembourg comprises almost a third of GDP and over a quarter in the Netherlands, underlining the importance of FDI for these small, open economies.

Sweden has also seen very rapid increases in FDI inflows in recent years. At US$ 5.4 billion in 1996, FDI inflows in Sweden are the sixth highest in Western Europe. Although Sweden has been a large source of FDI outflows for a number of years, it is only recently that incoming FDI became a major component of its domestic economy (as is true with other Scandinavian countries, particularly *Finland* and *Norway*).

By contrast, investment is of mixed importance in other Western European countries. Recent flows have accounted for high shares of GDP in countries such as Greece and Spain (where FDI stocks are considerable relative to other European countries). Perhaps most surprisingly given the size of its economy, FDI has been low in Italy, in terms of recent flows as well as cumulative stocks (Table 2.1).

The main investor countries in Western Europe have remained relatively constant over the last two decades. Traditionally, the main source of FDI in Western Europe has been the *US* (consistently the principal investing country), strongly followed by other European countries (both EU and EFTA countries have made extensive intra-EU investments). For example, when examining accumulated investment flows into the EU-12 bloc between 1984-93, the US was responsible for 33 percent and EFTA nations for 31 percent (Eurostat, 1995). The original and (largely) continuing reason for US companies investing in Western Europe is access to its markets - either the different national markets or more recently, the integrated EU Single Market. By 1995, Western Europe as a whole was the destination for 51 percent of total US direct investment abroad (US Department of Commerce, 1996). The ranking of countries in Western Europe has not altered significantly over the last two decades. In 1995, the main destination was the UK (17 percent of total US investment abroad), followed by Germany (6 percent), the Netherlands (5 percent) and Switzerland (5 percent).

More recently, *Japan* has emerged as a key investor country in Western Europe. In fact, its FDI flows into Europe grew the fastest during the 1980s. The number of Japanese manufacturing companies with production investments in Western Europe increased from 179 to 727 between 1983 and 1995. Although Japan's FDI in Western Europe is sizeable, it should be noted that it has been a less significant destination than the US - between 1990 and 1994, the EU only accounted for 20 percent of Japan's FDI, while the US received 50 percent (JETRO, 1996). In terms of flows, the UK has been the main destination, with 40 percent of cumulated EU-15 flows from Japan between 1951 and 1994, followed by the Netherlands (23 percent) and Germany (10 percent) (Eurostat, 1995).

Also in recent years, *Western European countries* themselves have become one of the principal sources of FDI in the region. With the industrial restructuring triggered by the Single Market programme and the enlargement of the EU, intra-European flows have risen substantially. For example, in the EU-12, intra-EU flows as a share of total investment grew from 28 percent in 1984-86 to 36 percent in 1991-93, though it has fallen off again in recent years (Eurostat, 1995). Lastly, it is important to draw attention to newer sources of FDI. As part of their rapid internationalisation, several *other Asian countries* have followed Japanese investors into Western Europe, particularly South Korean and Taiwanese investors. Some of the largest investments made in Western Europe in the

1990s have been made by companies from these countries, such as LG in Wales, Samsung in north-eastern England and Chung Wha in Scotland.

Statistics on the sectoral composition of FDI for Western Europe as a whole are not available, although data is available for the EU. Within the EU, the dominant element of FDI is tertiary investment - between 1984 and 1993, service sectors attracted 63 percent of new flows (Eurostat, 1995). Within services, the main sectors have been finance and banking, followed by real estate and trade, hotel and catering services. Within the industrial sector, the principal recipient manufacturing industries have been electronics (four percent of total 1991-93 EU-12 flows), chemicals (five percent) and transport equipment (five percent).

Locational Determinants of Foreign Investment in Western Europe

Flows in Western Europe rose faster than other parts of the world during the early 1980s and early 1990s as a result of increasing economic integration. Integration has been the product of several different, though distinct processes: the Single Market programme, the prospect of further European economic integration through EU monetary union, and the enlargement of the EU (especially with its extension to the east). In combination, these processes have not only generated larger flows into Western Europe as a whole, but they have catalysed substantial restructuring within the region as well.

Of these processes, the most important for FDI appears to have been *the Single Market programme*. This sought to make the EU economy more competitive through a process of market liberalisation and trade deregulation, primarily driven by the desire to make intra-EU trade and investment more efficient. The programme consisted of a series of measures designed to remove remaining non-tariff barriers to the free movement of goods, services, capital and labour within the Community, including: the harmonisation of technical standards between different Member States; greater rights of establishment and service provision for all EU-based companies in sectors such as financial services and road transport; liberalisation of national public procurement restrictions; and common rules on indirect taxation.

In order to become more competitive in this integrated marketplace, large European firms responded by investing and restructuring their operations in order to take account of this new market environment. Rather than having to organise their investment strategies around different EU markets, the production, distribution and administrative facilities of MNEs are being increasingly consolidated - often in separate locations - with a view to serving the Single Market as a whole.

The Single Market also stimulated FDI from outside the EU. The Single Market programme was perceived by some firms as a protectionist device which could potentially exclude firms based outside the EU, particularly as it took place at a time of increasing EU anti-dumping action against firms from the Far East. Consequently, a number of firms from the US, Japan and the rest of Western European set up operations within the EU to avoid exclusion from the emerging European marketplace.

Plans for *European Monetary Union* (EMU) has reinforced this trend, as companies are preparing for a market in which financial transactions will be eased by a common currency. Owing to its current unpredictable and political nature of its future, the full consequences of EMU for FDI flows is, once again, difficult to anticipate. When it commences, EMU will have the effect of increasing economic integration within the countries which participate in the first phase of EMU, which may in turn lead to some diversion of FDI from non-participating countries. Given that there is some empirical evidence to suggest that exchange rate volatility affects investment decisions (Cushman, 1985), EMU may indeed lead to some investors locating close to their final markets so that their costs and revenues are denominated in the same currency (Barrel and Pain, 1997).

At present, two consequences seem likely if EMU takes place. First, countries excluded from the process may be at a locational disadvantage compared to those inside the single currency area, owing to the reduced foreign exchange costs and lower transaction costs which will feature in EMU countries. Second, of all the countries in Western Europe not to proceed with EMU, possibly the biggest potential loser in terms of FDI could be the UK, which has been the largest single beneficiary of non-EU FDI in Western Europe. Some large foreign investors, such as Toyota Motor, have already publicly voiced their concerns over the possible consequences of their future investment plans in the UK were the country to remain outside the EMU. Some observers have warned that if the UK remained outside EMU, 'foreign investors whose primary markets are in continental Europe could have an incentive to locate there rather than in the UK' (Barrel and Pain, 1997).

Enlargement of the EU has been another major factor in encouraging investment flows. Enlargement has been taking place in several stages: through the expansion of the EU with membership by Sweden, Finland and Austria in 1995; with the increasing liberalisation of trade between the EU and EFTA through the European Economic Area agreement; and lastly, through the Europe Agreements on trade and the current membership negotiations with several Central and Eastern European countries.

Economic integration has largely determined the scale of flows into Western Europe. However, the scale and direction of flows within Western Europe have been shaped by a combination of different factors operating at different spatial and regulatory levels (Dicken, 1994). The locational determinants of FDI have been the subject of considerable conjecture in both policy-making and academic circles. The bulk of location studies tend to concentrate on the main factors which shape investment patterns at the national or regional level. In common with most surveys, an important study in Western Europe concluded that no 'one single overriding location factor' seemed to determine corporate location decision-making (CEC, 1993). Companies are generally looking for a combination of elements, and the outstanding attribute of a winning country/region is that it has the particular combination of characteristics that best satisfy the criteria of a specific project. In fact, there is a very considerable diversity in the key influences on location decisions between project types and between companies. All this confirms that the firm-specific nature of the location decision-making process and warns against generalisation. This issue is examined again from a policy perspective in Chapter 4.

Locational characteristics can be divided into price and non-price factors. According to some, non-cost, subjective factors, such as the quality of labour, are becoming more important owing to the increasing knowledge-based nature of production. This is in line with recent survey research which points to the growing importance of non-cost factors in determining the location decision making process. Nevertheless, cost or price-related locational factors cannot be completely ignored. Some surveys tend to underplay the significance of cost-related factors such as labour costs and financial incentives (Christodoulou, 1996).

Different factors also tend to predominate at different spatial scales (Table 2.2). At national level, market and customer proximity remain critical (though the processes of economic integration identified above have diminished its significance), as well as factors such as the quality of infrastructure. At regional level, additional factors are important, such as the availability of financial assistance and suitable sites. As economic integration reduces the importance of locating close to markets and customers in many industries, these other factors can assume more importance, not just in influencing the scale of investment, but the type as well. Rather than organising production, administration and distribution facilities on a national basis, companies are beginning to concentrate these functions in centralised locations in the EU. New patterns of FDI can be expected as different regions and countries not only demonstrate increasing specialisation in particular industries but also in specific business functions. As a result, the emerging patterns of foreign investment in the EU are increasingly shaped by the location requirements of specific corporate activities rather than whole companies, in which differences in production across the EU can be key in influencing decisions. These patterns are likely to remain volatile, as the further separation of different functions within multinationals could increase the mobility of foreign investment.

Attitudes to Foreign Investment Attraction

Against this background, national attitudes to the attraction of investment have become more positive. As elsewhere, the regulatory regimes operating in Western Europe's economies play a large role in determining the locational attractiveness of different countries. Governments can regulate FDI by different instruments, including: FDI pre-notification procedures; foreign exchange controls; aspects of national competition policy; and restrictions over foreign ownership of indigenous industry and commerce. Quite often these controls are applied to sensitive sectors such as financial services, energy and transport, though some restrictions on foreign mergers or acquisitions can affect FDI in all industrial sectors.

Table 2.2 Most important location factors for mobile investment in manufacturing in Europe during the 1980s

| Factors | Companies identifying factor as critical or important to choice of: | | | |
| | Country | | Region | |
	Critical	*Important*	*Critical*	*Important*
Business factors:				
- Proximity to markets	34	51	19	31
- Availability of raw materials & components	9	23	12	17
- Proximity to major customers	17	14	18	6
- Availability of site	5	5	17	17
National/ local characteristics:				
- Financial assistance	11	20	19	20
- Promotion/attitudes of government	6	19	9	23
- Official language/linguistic skills	-	-	-	-
- Corporate taxation	6	15	3	-
Labour factors:				
- General availability of labour	8	26	15	32
- Quality of labour	8	22	9	29
- Availability of skilled labour	9	19	11	22
- Labour relations	6	17	5	6
- Labour attitudes	8	14	0	17
Cost factors:				
- Cost of land/premises	5	17	11	18
- Cost of labour	11	22	9	17
Infrastructure:				
- Quality of road & rail services	23	20	15	32
- Proximity to port	8	11	6	15
- Proximity to major airports	9	14	6	31
- Quality of telecoms	5	12	2	11
Quality of life & personal factors:				
- Cultural factors	5	17	0	23
- Schools for expatriate children	2	11	2	9
- Educational facilities	0	6	2	12
- Overall attractiveness of area	5	6	6	8

Source: CEC, 1993.

Other common regulatory measures have not been used by individual Western European governments. The most obvious example are rules governing local content. Local content requirements can compel incoming investors in the manufacturing sector to source a certain proportion of their material and service needs within a given country or spatial area (seen in the case of the EU as a whole, as described in the following section). At national level, these measures have been generally eschewed in Western Europe for less interventionist approaches which aim to encourage local content by developing the surrounding local supplier infrastructure and supporting linkages between foreign investors and domestic companies.

Another such restriction concerns the numbers of expatriate employees staffing any given organisation. As with local content regulations, these controls are not used widely by Western European governments. In fact, some Western European countries are examining ways in which they can make it easier for companies to employ overseas nationals. Sweden, for example, has been examining its taxation system in order to allow tax breaks for foreign executives on limited duration posts in Sweden.

Over the last two decades, policy stances designed to control and limit foreign ownership in Europe's national economies have gradually given way to more positive attitudes towards FDI, contributing to the expansion of FDI in Western Europe (UNCTAD, 1995). Deregulation, demonopolisation, privatisation, and the reform of trade and foreign investment regimes have been central to the high levels of international direct investment in the 1990s (OECD, 1997a). In particular, there have been two key factors at national level which have contributed to increases in FDI in recent years: deregulation of foreign mergers and acquisition; and increasing privatisation and deregulation of monopolised industries.

Mergers and acquisitions (M&As) constitute the most common form of FDI, and their deregulation has been one of the main factors easing the process of FDI in advanced economies. Most governments are now liberalising their policies towards foreign M&As. Foreign companies have been given greater freedom in entering previously-restricted sectors in many Western European countries, in part as a result of deregulation at the EU level through the Single Market programme.

The second element of deregulatory change which has promoted FDI in Western Europe is the privatisation of former state-controlled assets.

The upsurge in privatisation throughout Western Europe is undoubtedly making more countries receptive towards incoming FDI, especially in sectors with little previous foreign involvement.

Although Western Europe in general presents a favourable and proactive FDI environment - as evidenced by the high volume of inward and outward flows - countries view the attraction of foreign investment with differing degrees of priority, both with respect to the impact on the national economy and as a contribution to solving regional economic problems. Broadly speaking, there is a division into three categories:

- countries that have long-standing policies aiming to maximise the benefits of FDI in regional and national economies;
- those countries that traditionally either distrust losing control of domestic economic activity to foreign enterprises, fear the risk of increased competition with local businesses or do not regard the benefits of FDI projects as justifying the costs of their promotion; and
- formerly hostile countries which have begun to pursue more positive policies.

Strong Promotion

Over the past decade, the most active countries in encouraging FDI have been Belgium, Ireland, the Netherlands, Spain and the UK. They have all been characterised by relatively deregulated approaches to foreign ownership within national economies and a range of policy instruments for attracting foreign investment projects. The importance placed on foreign investment has usually arisen either out of opportunity (as in the case of the UK and the Benelux countries, where their existing location advantages have guaranteed substantial interest by potential investors, especially from outside Western Europe) or the need to base national economic development on foreign investment (as in Ireland and Spain). In many ways, the best examples of this approach have been the UK and Ireland.

(i) The UK

The UK has traditionally had the most systematic approach to targeting and attracting foreign investment projects. The attraction of FDI has been an explicit objective of regional and industrial policies for nearly two decades, contributing to the UK having the largest share of all direct investment in Western Europe. US and Japanese investment has been particularly welcomed, allowing the UK to benefit from the surge of FDI into Western Europe catalysed by the Single Market programme. Foreign investment has been critical in the economic regeneration of certain regions, such as Scotland and Wales, where investment in the electronics sector led to the emergence of highly-competitive clusters of IT firms. Moreover, the UK has maintained one of the most liberal and active markets for corporate take-overs in Western Europe, so that a large share of the country's investment flows is accounted for by merger and acquisition activity.

A key measure in the UK's approach to FDI was the early liberalisation of foreign ownership regulations relative to other Western European countries. During the early 1980s, the UK actively sought to eliminate all its controls and regulations governing foreign investment in order to further encourage FDI. It was one of the first European countries to abolish foreign exchange controls. In addition, sectoral restrictions have been at a minimum and pre-authorisation procedures are absent.

Another factor has been the UK's ambitious privatisation programme - particularly in traditional state-controlled activities, such as public utilities (telecommunications, rail transport, electricity, water) - setting a trend which the much of Western Europe appears to be following to varying degrees. As a result of this deregulation and demonopolisation process, the UK has received FDI in sectors which were previously the domain of nationalised industries (eg. water, power supply and transport). The advanced nature of this process in the UK was accelerated by deregulation of its financial markets, notably with the 'Big Bang' in 1986 in which UK markets were opened up to foreign competition. Not only has this led to foreign investment increasing across British industry through a wave of M&As, but UK financial service firms captured a commanding share of the market for brokering M&As across Europe as a whole, making London the centre of such activity in Western Europe.

(ii) Ireland

Similar to the UK, Ireland has developed a well-organised industrial policy which places great emphasis on the attraction of foreign investment. Given the problems of high unemployment and the limited capabilities of domestic firms to expand, Ireland has looked to inward investment as the main source of employment creation for several decades. Foreign investment has consequently had a significant impact on the levels of exports, innovation, productivity and diversification within Irish industry, not just directly but through the knock-on effects on domestic supplier firms. The country's success in attracting projects - especially in the electronics and financial services sectors - can be attributed to a mix of its incentive advantages (eg. Ireland has been given special dispensation within European Commission rules to lower corporation tax, as described in Chapter 6), location factors such as a well-educated, compliant and relatively low-cost workforce and the operation of its inward investment organisation (IDA-Ireland).

Unlike the UK, Ireland continues to operate some policies which curtail FDI. For example, Ireland imposes some reciprocity considerations on investors from non-EU countries in certain sectors (eg. banking, finance and insurance). Another feature of the Irish economy which may limit FDI is the existence of state monopolies in certain sectors such as telecommunications, air transport and energy. This structural feature of the Irish economy is, however, in the process of change with privatisations recently taking place in the insurance and food sectors.

Weak Promotion

In contrast to this first category of policy attitudes, other countries have been either disinterested, or occasionally negative towards foreign investment. In particular, Germany, Italy and Switzerland have undertaken relatively little promotional activity; in some cases, there have even been expressions of antipathy towards the attraction of foreign firms.

(i) Germany

For Germany, overseas trade and investment promotion policies are pursued, but the need to encourage FDI has hitherto been doubted. Partly this has been due to the fact that Germany has historically been relatively successful in attracting investment without policy actions. However, while German agencies are far from averse to attracting FDI, there remains a widespread belief that foreign investment decisions are often not swayed by targeted marketing campaigns or financial inducements.

The country is a good example of how a relatively liberal environment does not necessarily influence FDI flows. The legal freedoms of foreign companies to take-over German firms are limited by the few opportunities that arise for doing so. This is mainly due to the country's industrial structure which is dominated by small and medium-sized enterprises and firms whose controlling ownership remains relatively stable as a result of bank or family ownership. At the end of 1995, only 678 domestic firms in Germany were publicly listed, compared with 1,971 enterprises in the UK (Bundesbank, 1997). The lack of publicly-quoted German companies prevents the acquisition of a major shareholding by foreign companies.

From a policy point of view, more attention is given to arresting the flow of German investment abroad by German manufacturing companies seeking sites of lower production costs, especially in Central and Eastern Europe. Nevertheless, greater efforts have been made recently to attract foreign investment into Germany - in June of this year, the German parliament passed legislation designed to speed planning procedures for industrial investments for greenfield sites (*Financial Times*, 1996a). Where inward investment promotion is active, it tends to be the responsibility of the individual *Länder* or local/municipal authorities, with very loose coordination provided by a central national agency.

(ii) Italy

Italian agencies have also been sceptical of the value of FDI in the past, and as a result, there are few policies to support its attraction. Structural differences between Italy and other European economies have reinforced this policy approach, as investors have been dissuaded by the mix of a large public sector and a private sector offering few acquisition opportunities because of the number of small companies and the underdeveloped stock market. Consequently, Italian industrial and regional policies have generally relied on national economic growth and the redistribution of domestic investment (especially to the *Mezzogiorno*), though the recent programme of privatisation and the introduction of new legislation for the promotion of FDI suggests that the attitudes of Italian authorities will change in future. For example, a number of the restrictions applied to foreign investment have been relaxed in sectors such as banking, transport, radio and television.

(iii) Switzerland

Switzerland is one of the most important sources of foreign investment, and the volume of outflows have far exceeded inward investment. Unlike Germany and Italy, this is perhaps less a result of policy decisions than a recognition that the country has relatively few location advantages. In terms of potential acquisitions, the Swiss manufacturing sector is dominated by small, family-run firms (similar to Italy), while the cantonal division of the country and the limited role of federal authorities has made the Swiss market less integrated than its European neighbours. Its refusal to take part in the European Economic Area free-trade zone has also sent signals to potential investors that Switzerland may be a poor location for serving a wider European market, while its own domestic market is too small to attract significant investment.

Promotion in Transition

The last category of countries is the largest: there are several countries which have been wary of foreign investment in the past, but are increasingly active in encouraging its attraction, of which France, the Scandinavian countries, and Greece and Portugal are especially prominent.

(i) France

Chief among these is France, which until the mid-1980s, displayed little enthusiasm for entry by foreign enterprises. Indeed, the former socialist government in the early 1980s was relatively inhospitable towards foreign investors, particularly those acquiring French businesses (Bailey, Harte and Sugden, 1991). However, over the past decade, French government policy appears to have experienced a 'sea change', in large part a response to the persistence of unemployment. Government agencies have been more energetic in bringing in FDI and the regulatory environment for foreign companies has been considerably relaxed. This has been reflected in the reorganisation of inward investment promotion activities within France, resulting in an expansion of the Invest in France network (with a staff of 74 - larger than that of the UK - and 17 overseas offices), and rewarded by the rapid rise in foreign investment in the country in the 1990s.

At the same time, extensive liberalisation of the country's investment regulations has been taking place. With the exception of defence, air and maritime transport, there are no longer widespread sectoral restrictions limiting foreign investment in France. Prior authorisation procedures have also been considerably relaxed and are now only necessary for investments that pose a threat to law and order and public safety. That said, France continues to impose reciprocity requirements in certain sectors (eg. telecommunications, audio-visual industries, publishing and hydrocarbons), especially on investors from outside the European Economic Area. In particular, a degree of wariness remains in allowing large domestic companies to pass into foreign ownership, as demonstrated by the government's recent blocking of a bid for part of the Thomson electronics group by Daewoo.

Other factors are also increasing the scope for foreign investment in the French economy. In this respect, financial deregulation and the government's vast privatisation programme are important. Although the process of privatisation has been slow and uneven, there could be significant opportunities for foreign investment in the telecommunications sector following the process of deregulation currently underway. In addition, France is gradually amending its corporate laws to allow greater scope for foreign companies to acquire domestic concerns (UNCTAD, 1995). In February 1996, for example, the French repealed a law that required prior authorisation for the acquisition of French enterprises by non-EEA investors.

(ii) Scandinavian countries

A more recent redirection of policy has taken place in the Scandinavian countries, which have all recently launched or are planning the establishment of government agencies with the specific remit of promoting themselves as FDI locations. In *Sweden*, long-standing inactivity with regards to FDI has ended as foreign investment is increasingly regarded as a potential means of reducing the country's rising unemployment. Until the early 1990s, Sweden had one of the most restrictive frameworks towards

FDI in Western Europe but has now instigated wide-ranging liberalisation. For example, in 1992, Sweden abolished the Law on the foreign acquisition of Swedish firms and also overturned the need for foreigners to get permission to transact business in the country. The country's recent accession to the EU has been a major factor in this process - similar to the surge in foreign investment into Portugal and Spain in the mid-to-late 1980s after these countries joined the Community. Other important factors in Sweden include a well-skilled workforce, favourable exchange rate and low corporation tax compared with the rest of the OECD (Blomstrom and Kokko, 1995).

The recent deep recession in *Finland* has prompted a reappraisal of attitudes to inward investment, just as its recent membership of the EU and trade opportunities in Russia have given the country a new attractiveness to foreign investors. Likewise, although not a member of the EU, closer integration within the European Economic Area has made *Norway* more sensitive to the importance of FDI and led to the removal of several restrictions on foreign ownership. Both countries have established inward investment promotion agencies for the first time in the 1990s.

(iii) Other Mediterranean countries

Changes in FDI policy in many West European countries are illustrated by parts of the Mediterranean area with formerly protective approaches to foreign ownership. This has been particularly true of the less-developed Member States of the EU, where continuing economic underdevelopment and the pressures of integration of trade, investment and production factors within the Single Market have combined to change attitudes to FDI. In *Portugal*, an intensive programme of liberalisation has opened up the country to foreign acquisitions, while the government is beginning to develop marketing tools, incentive policies and promotion agencies to attract FDI projects. As with Ireland and Spain, foreign investment is increasingly seen as a means of introducing modernisation into the country's industrial sectors through technology transfer and higher levels of productivity. The country is currently dismantling many of its sectoral restrictions on FDI (in areas such as water collection and distribution, banks and travel agencies, and basic sanitation services). Similarly, *Greece* has undergone transformation - again in large part, a response to greater integration within the EU - reflected in the recent establishment of Elke, a national inward investment agency intended to market the country abroad and coordinate foreign investor enquiries.

Community Regulation of Foreign Investment

Apart from national regulation, Community-wide policies affect foreign ownership and FDI flows. The regulation of foreign ownership is not a specific prerogative of the Community, but several fundamental areas of Community activity influence the entry and operation of non-national companies in the individual Member State economies.

The EU's approach to regulating FDI was largely established the initial principles in the Treaty of Rome. Under the Treaty, Article 52 allows freedom of establishment of nationals of one Member State within another Member State, including the formation of agencies, branches and subsidiaries. Furthermore, the European Court of Justice has ruled in several cases that Article 52 prohibits discrimination of such foreign-owned establishments by reason of nationality, ensuring that the freedom of foreign companies to invest in other countries and the equal treatment of foreign-owned and domestic businesses before the law would be applicable at least in the case of intra-EU investment (Wyatt and Dashwood, 1993). The Community has not extended its jurisdiction into other areas of foreign investment - such as national restrictions on foreign ownership of particular sectors - and in general, its role has been to encourage mutual recognition of different regulatory systems rather than the harmonisation of national rules. The Community's most important impact on foreign investment lies in the area of subsidy control, which is discussed in more detail in Chapter 4.

Community regulation effectively only covers the operation of Member State companies, but the principles applied here have formed the basis for the EU's stance in the negotiations for multilateral investment rules (CEC, 1995a). Empowered to act on behalf of the Member States in this area, the European Commission has favoured increasing global liberalisation of the regulations on FDI and foreign ownership. In its White Paper, *Growth, Competitiveness and Employment*, the Commission views the removal of barriers to direct investment as a key source of future EU growth, given the high share of outward and inward investment in its economic activity (CEC, 1994a). In developing a coherent position for the multilateral rules, the Commission endorsed five principles, recognising that some EU Member States would ultimately have to change their national regulations to comply (though not at this stage requiring them to do so):

- the legal right for foreigners to invest and operate in all economic sectors should be guaranteed;
- exceptions to this first principle should be narrowly and clearly defined and normally apply for national security reasons alone;
- discrimination between national establishments and foreign investors should not take place;
- no new discriminatory or restrictive practices should be introduced in these areas; and
- a commitment should be made to 'roll-back' measures not in keeping with these principles.

A further area where EU has been active is in developing a liberal FDI framework bilaterally with individual states, particularly with CEE countries. As already noted, foreign investment is regarded as a key source of restructuring and growth for the CEE economies, a trend which the EU wishes to encourage. As part of the Europe Agreements and its pre-accession negotiations with several CEE countries, a number of liberal measures have been agreed (CEC, 1995a):

- national treatment of domestic and foreign enterprises is to be reciprocal, but introduced asymmetrically, both in terms of their establishment as well as their operation (with the EU liberalising more quickly);
- capital transfers between subsidiary and parent companies - such as the transfer of dividends and repatriation of capital - are to be liberalised;
- CEE countries are to provide equivalent protection to intellectual, industrial and commercial property as in the EU; and
- CEE competition rules - especially with regards to state aids - are to be adapted to comply with the Treaty of Rome.

Similar measures have been included in EU agreements with Russia and developing countries.

At the same time as campaigning for a more liberal investment climate worldwide, the EU has also pursued illiberal policies with a strong FDI component. While not directly affecting issues of ownership, they did have a major influence on the surge of FDI into the region over the last decade. Community trade policy - particularly in the late 1980s - was actively used to restrict imports from Asian companies in certain competitive industries, resulting in some multinationals establishing plants within the Community to evade restrictions (*The Economist*, 1989). These measures were not initially intended to affect FDI strategies, but only to protect European companies from what was perceived to be predatory pricing. Hence, accusations of dumping - in which companies exporting to the Community are suspected of pricing their products below their 'normal value' in order to drive out local competition - were launched against companies (mainly Japanese) in industries such as printer manufacture. The imposition of anti-dumping duties on these imports prompted many companies to set up 'screwdriver' operations inside the Community, in which the bulk of components were imported for final assembly. However, the European Commission response to these tactics was to use trade policy to influence FDI strategies, at least with regards to the *type* of investment made. Although not operated at national level, EU local content rules were laid down to increase the percentage of local components used by the 'screwdriver' plants, notably for photocopier and VCR manufacturers. Moreover, rules of origin regulations were imposed to compel firms to transfer high-value added aspects of production to their European locations by applying anti-dumping rules in cases where the 'most technologically-sophisticated components' in a product were being imported into the Community.

Lastly, Community policy affecting FDI includes the regulatory liberalisation championed as part of the wider Single Market programme. Not only has the Single Market as a whole had a significant effect in promoting FDI into and within the EU, specific measures have led to the deregulation of capital flows between foreign-owned subsidiaries and EU parent companies. For example, a Commission Directive on the full liberalisation of capital movements between Member States came into effect by the mid-1990s, effectively concluding a period of capital liberalisation undertaken at different rates by Member States.

Institutional Framework for Foreign Investment Promotion

Growth in FDI has not only responded to (and in turn led to) greater regulatory liberalisation in FDI restrictions, but also to institutional approaches to encouraging and retaining foreign investment. The policies for attracting mobile investment projects are the subject of the second part of this study, but it is important to consider the organisations set up to promote investment. Nearly all Western European countries undertake promotional and aftercare services to attract foreign investment. In recent years, specialist inward investment agencies have proliferated at both national and regional levels, gaining greater institutional autonomy from other government departments and receiving an increasing share of FDI policy resources.

To understand how the activities of promotion agencies - particularly those associated with image-building and investment generation through incentive-based policy approaches - can be important, it is useful to outline certain features of the process of investment decision-making. Companies rarely make comprehensive and detailed examinations of their location requirements and the location options, but partially resort to 'satisficing', in which the process of finding the optimal location is set against the desire to find the first location to satisfy a set of key criteria. Where satisficing is an important if not dominant feature of the decision process, inward investment agencies (IIAs) not only have scope for influencing consideration of their region but can often be welcomed by providing a service to companies in simplifying the acquisition of the location information necessary for a decision.

The ability of IIAs to affect location decisions can be summarised in three stages, though in most cases, the different stages tend to operate in parallel. Agencies can raise *regional visibility* through promotional literature and directed campaigns targeting specific companies, in which the objective is put their region in contention for an investment project. Where serious interest is being shown in the region as a location, agencies can then supply an element of *regional certainty* by providing the company with the information it requires for the decision and addressing any questions or uncertainties. At the last stage, particularly where a large investment project is considering a few potential locations, competing investment agencies can target their promotional activities at individuals within the company - often by employing psychological factors such as hospitality - to demonstrate *regional commitment* to the project.

The institutional structure for attracting and developing FDI will clearly have a direct bearing on any given country's ability to achieve these objectives. In order to give a fuller picture of the role institutions play in attracting FDI, the following sub-sections examine: the organisational configuration of FDI institutions in Western Europe; the main promotional policy activities undertaken by inward investment agencies (IIAs); and lastly and separately, the role of local authorities (as they are often placed outside the main organisational structure for investment promotion).

The Organisation of Foreign Investment Promotion in Western Europe

Different Western European countries adopt a variety of institutional approaches towards inward investment promotion. Some Western European countries operate a highly centralised approach to inward investment, with central government handling all matters to do with incoming FDI. This can lead to a 'one-stop shop' approach with one agency dealing with all matters relating to foreign investment (such as incentives). On the other hand, some operate a highly decentralised approach which allows various actors (including sub-national agencies) to be involved in marketing locations and determining financial assistance. At another level, institutional approaches also differ in terms of how effectively inward investment attraction is managed - not least because IIAs vary greatly in their resources and strategic capabilities.

Broadly speaking, Western European countries fall into two different categories regarding their institutional structures for foreign investment promotion: countries with long-established structures; and countries only recently developing promotional organisations.

The *first* group are those with established institutions for FDI promotion. Countries in this group include the UK, Ireland, Spain, the Netherlands and Belgium. This group has long-established, well-coordinated structures for inward investment promotion and incentive decision-making. As a measure of their commitment to FDI attraction, it is worth noting that the largest IIAs in Western Europe tend to be located in these countries - hence, the Industrial Development Agency in Ireland employs 140 people in Ireland, while the Invest in Britain Bureau has a staff of approximately 60 (*Corporate Location*, 1996b).

These countries have effective systems for targeting potential investors, promoting the country and individual regions as inward investment locations, and coordinating the assembly of incentives packages for specific projects. These systems are normally coordinated through a central national agency that acts as a 'one-stop shop' for potential investors, often in collaboration with strong regional agencies in the case of the larger countries. In Belgium, the regional agencies are so strong that there is no national agency (reflecting the country's overall level of decentralisation).

Of all the countries in this group, the UK has the most elaborate and unique system which includes a very extensive network of personnel engaged in FDI promotion, coupled with a highly complex, overlapping structure for FDI promotion. This involves one national coordinating body, three powerful regional IIAs and eight English Regional Development Agencies. The Invest in Britain Bureau (IBB) is top of the overall promotional hierarchy in the UK. It undertakes promotional efforts for the whole of the UK through the British Embassies, High Commissions and Consulates-General. It also coordinates the activities of the various regional tiers below.

Extensive decentralisation of marketing is granted to certain regional IIAs. The three key IIAs are: Locate in Scotland (LIS - within Scottish Enterprise, the regional development agency responsible for Scotland), the investment arm of the Welsh Development Agency and the Industrial Development Board for Northern Ireland. They represent well-defined and relatively cohesive national entities with a wide range of additional economic development functions. Each has significant budgetary resources, even when compared with the national body in charge of FDI promotion, the IBB. For example, Locate in Scotland employs over 100 people (at a cost of approximately US$ 10 million in 1996-97) and had an operating expenditure of about US$ 40 million in the financial year ending in March 1997 (Scottish Enterprise, 1997). At the same time, incentive award responsibilities have been decentralised to the Scottish, Welsh and Northern Ireland Office. Such has been the competition for FDI between these well-equipped IIAs in the UK that the IBB occasionally has to arbitrate between them over the degree of competition exerted to win new projects, especially between Scotland and Wales.

English regions are not presently covered by agencies with these powers, although some have more limited regional development agencies. They have much smaller budgets and staff levels, and a narrower operational remit than agencies like LIS. In recognition of this disparity, the IBB established the English Unit within the DTI, which resulted in new investment offices being opened in Taiwan and South Korea dedicated to serving the promotional efforts of English regions (Christodoulou, 1996). The regional development agencies currently being created in England by the new Labour government may change this situation. Below this level, some local authorities play a limited role in FDI promotion but this occurs on an *ad hoc* basis, often augmenting the efforts of the national and regional IIAs. (Their policy initiatives are considered in a section below.)

The *second* group of Western European countries are those with less well-developed institutional arrangements for FDI promotion. This group includes countries which were formerly hostile towards FDI but are now attempting to seize a larger proportion of incoming investment. Examples within this group include France, Portugal and most Scandinavian countries. Although procedures vary, most of these countries have weakly coordinated mechanisms for uniting the various actors involved in the process of designing packages for incoming companies. The size of IIAs in these countries is also less than the first group of countries. For example, Portugal's FDI promotion agency employs 37 employees while Finland's employs a mere 3 people (*Corporate Location*, 1996b). Furthermore, most of these countries have few or no regional IIAs.

Some countries within this group, such as France, are now beginning to develop more effective institutional mechanisms for promoting FDI, including well-resourced IIAs. Indeed, France has been steadily strengthening its FDI promotional capabilities over the last decade or so. In 1992, the post of Ambassador-Delegate for international investment was established to promote foreign investment prospecting on behalf of French authorities. This augmented the existing work done by the Invest in France Network (IFN) and the Invest in France Agencies which have a number of overseas offices. In addition, France established a Foreign Investment Observatory to investigate foreign-owned companies and to aid the process of FDI promotion undertaken by the IFN. France now has a single, consistent policy for promoting foreign investment.

Other countries in this group are less well-established in the field of FDI promotion. Of these countries, the Scandinavian economies have the newest institutions for promoting FDI. The Invest in Sweden Agency (ISA) was only established in 1996; it employs 12 staff, but has additional representatives in overseas Chambers of Commerce, Trade Councils and Foreign Embassies.

It is clearly difficult to determine causality between the nature and scope of FDI promotional agencies and their ultimate success in attracting foreign investment. However, it does appear to be the case that institutional effectiveness plays some role in attracting incoming investment. Using the UK as an example, the fact that the bulk of FDI is directed towards areas which have the largest and best-resourced IIAs (especially Scotland and Wales) seems to indicate this link. Further, the well-established IIAs (and related development agencies) are also those that have had the most success in developing and embedding FDI through targeted aftercare activities designed to promote re-investment (see, for example, Amin and Tomaney, 1995).

The Main Promotional Activities Undertaken by IIAs

The main activities and functions of FDI agencies are set out in Table 2.3, though it is important to note that not all IIAs undertake all of the functions; cases of agencies being involved in policy formulation, for instance, are rare. Incentive awards also tend to be the prerogative of mainstream government departments. Traditionally, most of the work done by IIAs has been investment promotion. Wells and Wint (1990) have identified three different types of investment promotion activity commonly undertaken by IIAs. The first is *image-building* which is designed to improve the perception of a country or region as a location for investment. The second is *investment-generating activity* with promotional techniques being used to identify and contact key decision-makers in investing companies. The third is *post-investment service* techniques which are designed to nourish and develop the investment once the company is established in the hope of securing secondary investments. Research examining the work of IIAs throughout Europe has shown that the main emphasis of most agencies is very much the promotional activities to attract the initial investment rather than post-investment services such as FDI *aftercare* policies (Young and Hood, 1994).

Table 2.3 Functions of foreign direct investment agencies

Policy formulation	Guidelines for FDI policy; assessment of the effectiveness of policy; integration with national and regional industrial policies
Investment promotion and attraction	Marketing information and intelligence; marketing planning; marketing operations outside and inside the country
Investment approvals	Screening and evaluation of potential projects
Granting of incentives	Consideration of incentive offers; incentive negotiations; incentive approvals. Includes also financial incentives, land and buildings etc.
Providing assistance	Includes assistance with public utilities (roads, water, electricity, sewerage, telecommunications), factories and training links with universities and research institutes, identification of potential suppliers
Monitoring; aftercare services	Continuation of assistance post-launch. Liaison for possible expansion projects, developing local suppliers etc.

Source: Young and Hood, 1994.

The main focus of these activities is competition with neighbouring countries and regions in Western Europe, rather than with other parts of the world. Agencies tend to design their promotional policies to attract projects that are already destined for Western Europe, though this may change with increasing competition from CEE countries for investment. As a result of this emphasis on European competition, a key element underpinning the investment promotion activity of IIAs has been the issue of targeting.

In this respect, sectoral targeting has become key. Although most IIAs base their FDI targeting strategy on existing sectoral clusters in the host economy (using analytical techniques such as location quotients and shift share analysis), some targeting undertaken by IIAs is less structured. Countries and regions generally target the same sectors, not least because of their locational mobility. Therefore, manufacturing sectors, such as electronics and pharmaceuticals, feature strongly as FDI target sectors owing to the international mobility of these sectors. Some regions, such as Rhône-Alpes, seek to attract higher-quality, R&D-related FDI which can augment their indigenous capabilities in any given field (eg. precision engineering). Similarities between targeting strategies mean that the competition for the available investment in these sectors is intense.

A good example of sectoral targeting by IIAs is the approach taken by LIS towards the electronics industry in Scotland. In the year to March 1997, electronics projects accounted for 20 percent of the total number of new FDI projects, 83 percent of the planned investment and 38 percent of planned jobs (LIS, 1997). Sectoral targeting enables the host economy to obtain agglomeration economies in terms of local skills resources, local suppliers and R&D (Brown *et al*, 1997). However, some commentators have warned that regions should not be too dependent upon on any one sector because of the potential problems of industrial restructuring in the future (CEC, 1993).

Some observers have recently advocated that IIAs should take a more strategic approach towards FDI attraction and target sectors that show the greatest economic benefits suitable for the host region (Young, Hood and Wilson, 1994). The range of impact indicators should also go beyond simply employment creation to consideration of other indicators, including measures of technology transfer, supplier linkages and export potential. Although this seems a useful approach which could lead to more strategic decision-making concerning the suitability of FDI for host economies, most IIAs continue to seek FDI in their targeted sectors, often with limited consideration of the potential impact on the host economy.

As noted above, the role given to the third investment promotion activity undertaken by IIAs (ie. post-investment services or aftercare) generally receives less attention. Patently, FDI aftercare strategies become more important as the amount of greenfield FDI diminishes and competition for expansion investment intensifies. Indeed, there is already some empirical evidence to suggest that mature FDI locations in Western Europe are paying more attention to upgrading and developing existing foreign investors. For example, in 1995, the IBB established an initiative called the International Investor Development Programme in the UK. This programme targets the top 1,000 foreign investors in the UK and is specifically designed to enhance the status and autonomy of these companies (in order to generate future plant expansions and reduce the threat of possible closure) and to maximise the quality of these investment in terms of its supplier linkages and training. Aftercare policies are also being developed in the newer IIAs in Scandinavia (eg. Invest in Sweden).

Local Authorities and Inward Investment Promotion

Although local authorities have a limited role in inward investment promotion, their role has increased in recent years. Information on the scale of their FDI promotion is scanty and their activities are considered supplementary to the national efforts and consequently go largely unregistered and unmonitored. As a result, their contribution to overall policy competition is difficult to gauge. Nevertheless, it is possible to identify the type of policies they pursue, as local authorities are often responsible for measures not undertaken by other governmental organisations. In general, local assistance is viewed as having a key role in the later stages of inward investment promotion, as a way of providing an additional incentive to potential investors after the main financial incentive package has been offered. Rarely does the value of this assistance rival the amounts provided through the main incentive schemes, but local packages sometimes augment a location's chances in competition for a significant mobile investment project.

Normally these incentives take the form of a subsidy of part of an investment establishment. Two types of support are used commonly in Western European countries: labour market subsidies and property concessions. With regards to *labour market support*, training and employment assistance is regarded as the most important form of local measure. In many cases, this reflects the allocation of responsibilities of employment training to locally-based agencies. For example, in the UK, training assistance is provided by the Training and Enterprise Councils (in England and Wales) and Local Enterprise Companies (in Scotland), which were originally established to deliver such measures at a local level. These local agencies are frequently brought into negotiations with a foreign investor at a later stage, so that the financial package on offer could be supplemented by labour market financial support. Such assistance is becoming more valuable in the view of some policy-makers as the costs of creating a highly-skilled workforce for new investments have increased for many companies.

Although not strictly speaking a form of direct financial support, the provision of subsidised *property* and the preparation of potential sites have been important local instruments of FDI promotion. As with other local sources of support, property offers are normally made by local authorities in collaboration with the (national) agencies overseeing FDI negotiations. However, it has also been an effective tool for local authorities acting independently in attracting foreign investment, especially those that are outside designated aid areas and therefore cannot qualify for the direct financial incentives discussed above.

Conclusions

Over the past decade, Western Europe has experienced a steady increase in FDI, reinforcing its position as the primary global recipient of foreign investment. Increasing investment flows are a result of a variety of factors, especially increasing European integration. Although FDI flows fluctuate, the trends seem to exhibit a relatively fixed pattern over the long term, with the UK continuing to capture the main share. For most of Western Europe, the sectoral composition of FDI is heavily concentrated in the tertiary sector (particularly financial services), and parts of the secondary sector (especially high-technology sectors such as electronics, electrical engineering and chemicals).

Western European countries give varying priorities to the attraction of foreign investment as a policy goal. Over the last two decades, the trend has been towards creating more favourable environments for foreign investors and becoming more active in capturing mobile investment projects. While countries such as the UK and Ireland have long taken the lead in FDI promotion, most European countries have developed policies and institutions dedicated to attracting FDI. Germany, Italy and Switzerland have traditionally placed minimal importance on FDI policy.

The overall attitudes to the attraction of FDI can be seen in the increasing openness of European economies to foreign ownership. Greater liberalisation has taken place through a combination of widespread deregulation of restrictions on foreign investment and the privatisation of previously state-controlled parts of the economy (such as public utilities). Again, the UK has had a prominent part in this process, though the trends are pan-European. The latter point is evident from the EU's increasing role in this area, both by encouraging trade and capital liberalisation in the Single Market programme and in coordinating Member State negotiating stances on global and bilateral investment rules frameworks.

Increasing interest in FDI policy is also apparent in the creation of specific government agencies for promoting FDI. Variations exist on the organisational structure of FDI promotion in Western Europe - especially the extent to which regions have policy responsibilities - but there is a convergence in the types of policies operated by agencies and the increasing scope of their activities. The promotional activities of IIAs have widened from traditional marketing of a country/region to include more sophisticated targeting of specific sectors (and indeed, companies) as well as providing aftercare services to existing investors in order to secure future, expansion investments. Local authorities have an increasingly visible role in FDI promotion, often utilising a different, but complementary set of policies to those implemented by national organisations.

3 FDI Policy Approaches in Central and Eastern Europe

EWA HELINSKA-HUGHES AND MICHAEL HUGHES

Introduction

The purpose of this chapter is to highlight some of the issues concerning policy towards FDI in Central and Eastern Europe (CEE) within the context of the fundamental economic and socio-political transition which the region as a whole is experiencing. The relatively recent and dramatic array of changes will continue, affecting both the transition economies themselves and their economic relationships with the rest of the world, particularly their European neighbours. The most fundamental aspect of the reconfiguration of trade and investment relations will result from the completion of the next stage of EU enlargement which is expected to envelop the Czech Republic, Estonia, Hungary, Poland, Slovenia and Cyprus. The CEE dimension of enlargement will confront Western corporations with difficult choices concerning potential relocation of production and supply of products and services as market proximity and cost factors begin to clash with Community regulatory measures (Tucker, 1996). Therefore, policy competition for FDI will need to take on board a complex range of shifting corporate as well as national objectives (Lorenz, 1997; Parsley, 1997). As competition increases for FDI, where basic factor costs and advantages are comparable, corporate location decisions are likely to favour the more attractive incentive packages. Some confusion and ill feeling has already been generated by the scramble for large inward investment projects in Europe (Barnard, 1997).

It could be argued that almost all aspects of government policy can influence inward investment in CEE. Given the scale of economic and political reform in the CEE countries, a range of measures can have clear impacts on location decisions, including, *inter alia,* stabilising the legal environment (especially with respect to property ownership and licensing), environmental policy (as described in the chapter below), transport policy, housing provision and indeed, the overall running of the economy. The continuing perception of economic and political instability among potential investors in CEE means that any government efforts to reduce the uncertainty of investing and operating in different CEE business environments will influence location decisions.

Given this proviso that CEE governments are sensitive to how different policy areas influence inward investment decision, this chapter will concentrate on a select range of policies - ie. those designed to promote inward investment explicitly. In addition, it focuses mainly on the four Visegrad economies. These have all had different experiences with regards to FDI and illustrate the considerable variations and disparities between economies and regions resulting from the volume, nature and location of FDI. The role of FDI in transition economies is the subject of debate regarding both the process of privatisation and longer-term effects on economic development. According to Stankovsky (1995), 'Foreign Direct Investment is one of the main factors assisting in the transformation of eastern Europe from command to successful market economies'. However, a major study for UNCTAD (1995) points out that the participation of FDI in the transition process 'has been important, but mostly in a supportive manner, with this role varying greatly from country to country'.

Although a number of policy issues arise when examining FDI, particularly at levels where attraction measures are best implemented, it must be noted that the legacy inherited from the period when these economies were centrally planned is dominant. These affect each phase of FDI strategy for corporations and national and local political authorities, and subsequently the formation of attraction policy. Moreover, given the diversity of economic, political and social conditions prevailing in CEE, and the continuing state of flux, the observations in this chapter must be regarded as preliminary and tentative.

FDI Trends in CEE

Foreign investment has been given a strong impetus by economic reform in the transition countries. Their economies require sources of foreign capital for the replacement of much of their obsolete industrial machinery due to the lack of sufficient domestic investment and the desire to avoid escalating foreign debt. FDI is regarded as a major factor in a range of restructuring processes, including the transformation of ownership and corporate governance through privatisation, and the related aim of demonopolisation (Gray, 1996). Wider national economic policy objectives are also linked to foreign investor participation in terms of employment, export potential, contribution to regional development and spillover effects for domestic producers and suppliers.

It has been expected that foreign investors would provide important management and production skills training, eventually facilitating technology transfer. Thus, the transfer of both hard and soft technology via FDI with direct effects stemming from the presence of an enterprise in the economy is an important but relatively recent phenomenon. Prior to the post-1989 transition phase, CEE relied primarily upon various forms of trans-border cooperation with the West, especially through a limited number of joint ventures and licensing agreements, which were rather ineffective for know-how acquisition, boosting output, efficiency gains or developing markets for 'new' products.

FDI is frequently reported and analysed statistically at an aggregate level and viewed as a uniform feature within macroeconomic policy. However, this approach overlooks and devalues the crucial issues of modes and methods of FDI entry, their impact and possible 'lifespan'. These are important considerations when assessing the value of contributions to a host economy made by corporations according to their entry mode choice and the possible negative effects (Williams, 1997). Thus, there are also important matters for governmental strategists to address when formulating or revising FDI attraction policy. The quality and value-added dimension of different types of investment mode must be carefully considered and incorporated into economic development policy where the government is in a position to determine such a policy framework. When assessing the relative merits of investment projects and the need to establish outcome targets, attention should be given to corporate objectives and how these will contribute positively to those of the host economy. Impact analysis should take account of human as well as physical infrastructure development, such as: employee skill acquisition; wage rates; regional migration patterns; the degree of indigenisation of middle and senior management; and the effects upon domestic producers and suppliers including displacement potential, supply chain formation, regional industrial clusters, and spillover and demonstration effects.

Given these caveats about consideration of FDI at a macro level and the fact that statistical sources differ in their estimates of FDI stocks (as described in more detail in the Appendix), the scale of the increase in FDI in CEE is clear. For example, at the end of 1989, cumulative foreign investment was approximately US$ 2.5 billion (UN ECE, 1994), but by June 1998 this had risen to US$ 75.1 billion (PAIZ, 1998; Business Central Europe, 1998). Nevertheless, the amount of investment is small relative to other economies in Western Europe.

When looking at cumulative flows of FDI in 1995, the biggest recipients were Hungary and Poland, followed by the Czech Republic. Based on information supplied by UNCTAD, FDI to Eastern Europe fell between 1995 and 1996. Poland has the largest share of FDI inflows into CEE, attracting US$ 5.2 billion in 1996 (compared with US$ 2.5 billion in 1995). Next were Hungary with US$ 2 billion (down from US$ 3.5 billion) and the Czech Republic with US$ 1.2 billion (down from US$ 2.5 billion).

Hungary has been the main host country for foreign investment in the CEE. Not only has it received the largest share in aggregate terms, but FDI as a proportion of GDP is also greatest there (Table 3.1). It also has the highest figure of FDI per capita in CEE. The prominence of Hungary in FDI is at odds with its relatively low importance in trade terms. However this success in attracting FDI can be explained by its possession of several advantages, enabling the country to be an early primary location for foreign investment in the transition economies, a position which it has been able to reinforce over time (Hardy, 1994; Houde, 1994). First, Hungary was the first transition country to deregulate its controls on foreign ownership and investment. Second, successful and early implementation of widespread privatisation of its economy attracted a number of foreign investors through acquisition of state firms. Third, the country has often been cited in surveys of foreign investors as having the most consistent economic and political stability in the region. Lastly, its proximity to major Western European markets - notably Germany and Austria - also allows inward investors quick access to lucrative adjacent markets.

Hungary has been followed by Poland, which is currently experiencing rapid growth in FDI as compared with the other Visegrad countries (Table 3.1). According to Dresdner Bank (*Boss Export-Import*, 1996), the following factors have assisted in attracting foreign investment to Poland: market size, transfer of profits, liberal economic policy, privatisation, bilateral trading links, EU Association Agreement, changes in legislation bringing it closer to the EU norms, spare industrial capacity, geographical proximity to Germany, well-qualified and relatively low-cost labour force and a possibility of using Poland as a bridge for the Commonwealth of Independent States. Nevertheless, in per capita terms and as a share of total economic output, Poland remains behind many other CEE countries in terms of its potential for attracting FDI.

In terms of source countries, the EU and the US feature strongest in the FDI profiles of transition countries. Although the size of its flows to CEE are small relative to the size of the US economy (and its other outward flows), the US investment presence still contrasts markedly with its low level of trade with the transition countries. In contrast, Japan and other East Asian countries - traditionally large investors in Western Europe - have been slow to set up in the transition countries, though some large companies - such as Suzuki in Hungary and Daewoo in Romania and Poland - have begun to establish subsidiaries. Mention should also be made of the presence of international lenders - such as the European Bank of Reconstruction and Development - which have been important in financing development projects throughout the region, particularly in Poland.

FDI seems to be concentrated in certain manufacturing sectors, such as the automotive industry, food and drink, and telecommunications. This can be largely attributed to two sets of factors. First, FDI transactions in the region often constitute huge purchases by foreign companies (*Business Central Europe*, 1995). For example, the stock of FDI in the Czech road vehicles sector is dominated by the acquisition of, and subsequent investments in, the Czech car company Skoda by the German firm, Volkswagen. The Volkswagen investments of US$ 700 million represented nearly a quarter of the total FDI stock in the Czech Republic by the end of

1993. Second, privatisation programmes in the different countries have largely determined which sectors have received the most FDI. The select privatisation of parts of the economies has attracted significant amounts of foreign capital into certain sectors, such as food and telecommunications. Delays in initiating a large-scale privatisation programme in Poland stifled FDI until recently. For example, by the mid-1990s, less than five percent of total FDI took the form of foreign acquisitions of state-owned enterprises in Poland, with the majority of investment taking place through greenfields and joint ventures with existing firms, as compared to many other CEE countries (*Business Central Europe*, 1995).

Table 3.1 FDI comparisons in CEE

Country	FDI flows 1995 (US$ bn)	Per capita 1995 (US$)	1995 flows as % GNP [1]	FDI stocks end-1995 (US$ bn)	FDI stocks mid-1998 (US$ bn)	Per capita mid-1996 (US$)
Czech Rep.	2.5	242	6.9	5.8	7.8	597.3
Hungary	3.5	431	10.7	10.7	18	1,276.8
Slovenia	0.1	72	1	1.2	2.4	600.0
Slovakia	0.2	34	1.4	0.7	1.4	137.0
Poland	2.5	65	2.7	8.5	25.6	272.4
Romania	0.4	18	1.4	1.6	2.8	75.2
Estonia	0.2	138	8.8	0.5	1.3	377.5
Lithuania	0.04	11	1	0.4	1.0	97.4
Latvia	0.3	87	6.3	0.4	1.9	185.2
Bulgaria	0.1	14	1.1	0.5	1.3	68.4
Russia	1.5	9.7	0.3	5.5	10.3	39.9
Belarus	0.007	1	0.6	0.4	0.4^2	39.6
Moldowa	0.05	11	4.5	0.05	0.06^2	13.8
Ukraine	0.2	3	0.4	0.7	1.0^2	19.0

[1] FDI inflow in 1995, GNP from 1994, [2] 1996 figures

Sources: Ecoinform 1996 (various issues), Business Central Europe, Stan i Prognoza Koniunktury Gospodarczej Polski, Biuletyn No 9. 1996, Gdansk Institute of Market Research and Economic Survey for Europe in 1995-1996, ECE/UN Geneva; World Investment Report, UNCTAD, New York, Geneva 1996; PAIZ, 1998.

With respect to the motives of foreign investors in CEE, these can be divided into two overlapping categories (Halpern, 1995; Dunning, 1993). First, investors have been attracted by the prospect of the costs of skilled labour being relatively cheap compared to Western Europe. CEE locations appear to provide Western companies with the opportunity of setting up low-cost, manufacturing assembly operations in combination with good access to Western European markets. This has combined with the profusion of acquisition opportunities resulting from the mass privatisation programmes undertaken in nearly all CEE countries. However, the most desirable acquisition and joint venture opportunities are drying up fast, so greenfield site projects are likely to become FDI attraction policy targets (Hughes and Helinska-Hughes, 1997).

Second, and more importantly, CEE countries present Western companies with expanding consumer and industrial markets for which direct investment is often seen as a way of establishing a strong market presence. Surveys of Western investors in CEE suggest that market access and potential are more important factors than cheaper production costs - for example, the OECD found 44 percent of its survey respondents had invested to enter domestic markets, but only 9 percent had done so for resource-oriented reasons (CCET, 1994).

The Emergence of FDI Promotion in CEE

In general, there is a very high level of competition between and within CEE economies; national and local governments clearly see FDI as a major factor in the successful transition to a market economy. Therefore, they wish to capture large investment projects in order to benefit from the range of spin-off effects, particularly in areas where there is a serious unemployment problem or anticipated decline in economic activity. In addition, most CEE governments still regard FDI as an important plank in their privatisation policy.

However, much of this competition only becomes visible with high-profile inward investments where the politics of the situation highlight the issue but obscure the detail. Much of the competitive dynamics in these cases are shrouded in *ad hoc* deals. By the end of this decade, it is likely that competition will become far more ferocious as the 'cherry-picking' acquisitions and joint ventures disappear, and CEE economies are forced to compete between themselves and other emerging economies for declining volumes of FDI flows.

Therefore, one would argue that competition is not obviously direct at present, but it would appear that national-level negotiations do involve considerable 'stake-raising' offers. It is also important to recognise the detrimental effects that competition can have within countries where nationally-determined economic development policy can be undermined by local interests and corporate focused strategy can play off competing location and development agencies within and between countries.

With regards to policy instruments for attracting FDI, of all CEE countries, the earliest and most active in FDI promotion have been the Visegrad countries. Each varies in its approach to FDI attraction. It is perhaps too early to judge the impact of these policies but there are clear disparities between countries and regions. This is partly due to the variation in 'legacy' problems concerning physical and human infrastructure, economic structure of regions and market access which policies attempt to address through FDI with varying degrees of success.

CEE countries use a variety of measures in order to attract foreign investment (Stankovsky, 1995). Table 3.2 summarises various concessions available to potential foreign investors. By and large, they refer to tax concessions, reductions dependant upon fulfilment of various conditions and customs incentives, showing how extensive the use of tax is in CEE countries (and the similarity of this approach across all the countries). Some of the Visegrad countries offer limited tax-free holidays, but national governments and local administrations in all four countries offer a range of generous concessions to strategic investors.

The provision of incentives in itself is not enough to encourage FDI. Unlike Western Europe, it is usually more important to identify and remove impediments to investment within the existing tax system (OECD, 1995). As tax laws in most of the countries in the region still partly reflect the solutions adopted under communism, substantial changes are needed. In order for tax laws to comply with OECD rules, several aspects have to be in place including: depreciation of assets; treatment of expenses; rules concerning the way business losses are carried over; the transparency of the tax law; and taxes on business inputs, property and other non-income bases (Holland and Owens, 1995).

Tax concessions are offered in all Visegrad countries, the Czech government recently approving a seven-point package of investment incentives in April 1998. Czech authorities had declined to offer tax breaks or cut-price land, assuming that the country's strong, industrialised economy and close proximity to Western Europe was enough to secure major FDI inflows. However, major speculative attempts directed against the koruna in May 1997, followed by devaluation, led to a rethink of the policy towards foreign investment attraction. The subsequent reversal of the Czech government's policy in this respect in order to secure an investment of up to US$ 500 million by Intel, the US computer component manufacturer, proved to be the catalyst for a major change in its position in 1998 in response to increasing competition for inward FDI.

Perhaps the most advanced FDI promotion system in CEE is in Poland, which can be used as an example of typical features in the CEE policy approach. In 1991, the Polish government established the Industrial Development Agency (ARP) which acts as an investment agency and plays a major role in managing special economic zones (SEZs). The establishment of SEZs in Poland - based on the Act for Special Economic Zones passed by the Polish parliament in 1994 - demonstrates the importance of locally-available and spatially-specific incentives. To begin with, there were three SEZs in operation: Katowice, Suwalki and Euro-Park Mielec, with all SEZs designed to function for a period of 20 years. In 1997 new SEZs were established, among others, in Suwalki, Walbrzych, Legnica and Zgierz-Pabianice-Lodz. Currently, there are 17 SEZ operating or being set up in Poland.

The main incentives offered to investors in Polish SEZs include:
- 100 percent corporate income tax relief for the zone's first ten years of operation, falling to 50 percent over the next ten years or less;
- exemption from real estate tax for the duration of the zone (minimum of ten years);
- increased rate of fixed assets depreciation;
- exemption from customs duty on capital goods so long as ownership does not change within three years;
- recovery of VAT on imported fixed assets.

In order to benefit from the above incentives, companies must invest a minimum of MECU 2 in the case of Euro-Park Mielec and Katowice, and

ECU 350,000 in Suwalki. In terms of job creation, a potential investor has to employ a minimum of 100 people in Mielec and Katowice and 40 people in Suwalki. Each of the three zones offers particular advantages; Table 3.3 summarises the terms of tax exemption in the SEZ at Mielec.

The SEZ in Katowice was established in June 1996 within the framework of the 'Contract for Silesia'. It covers an area of 827 ha. in south-western Poland and comprises four sub-zones: Gliwice, Jastrzebie Zdroj, Sosnowiec-Dabrowa-Gornicza and Tychy. The main assets of the area are a well-developed infrastructure and transportation network, and an almost unlimited supply of highly-qualified labour. Strategic investors already committed to the area include a new Opel car factory valued at US$ 300 million which is expected to create 2,000 jobs. One of the world's largest car spare parts manufactures - Delphi Automotive Systems - is due to invest US$ 30 million there in 1998.

Table 3.3 Tax exemptions in Special Economic Zone Mielec

Terms of exemption	Period	Tax-exempt income
Investment up to MECU 2	Until the entire invested amount is deducted	Amount equal to the investment's value
Investment above MECU 2	The first 10 years The remaining period	100 percent 50 percent
Creation of new jobs	The first 10 years The remaining period	10 percent for every 10 new employees 5 percent for every 10 new employees
Export	The first 10 years The remaining period	Amount equal to 50 percent of export revenue Amount equal to 25 percent of export revenue

Source: information supplied by the Polish Agency for Foreign Investment

Recently, Isuzu of Japan decided to locate a diesel engine plant in Poland; a total investment of $240 million creating 650 jobs (PIAZ, 1997). The company chose Poland in preference to the West Midlands in the UK. According to Robert Hayman-Collins, director of West Midlands

Development Agency 'the Poles put a lot of money on the table - the UK does not do that very much, in spite of impressions of the country' (Groom, 1997). However, competition for inward investment is keen and local development agencies frequently act on their own discretion (Murdoch, 1997).

Future Investment Trends in CEE

After 1989, CEE countries can be viewed as possible alternative locations to domestic investment by Western European companies and posing a further strategic option for transnational corporations. All of the transition economies are acutely aware of the competitive pressures for attracting FDI, and they are convinced that such external influences play a fundamental role in socio-economic development. Consequently, according to their respective budgetary resources, CEE governments have devoted funds to improve their institutional infrastructure for assisting FDI at national and local levels. There is a clear recognition that administrative problems as well as economic conditions seriously impede FDI. Hence, they have more directly focused capital expenditure and privatisation initiatives towards alleviating the massive shortcomings of basic infrastructure provision and administrative support.

Due to the disparities of sheer size, legacy problems of regional and sectoral underdevelopment, and variation in natural and human capital endowment, the CEE countries present different 'attractiveness and risk ratings' according to both economic criteria and perceived corporate/managerial advantage. These criteria appear to be axiomatic within the literature and comprise features upon which the various country specific factors can be ranked. Notwithstanding the various assessments currently undertaken, it is already apparent that these rankings will change significantly as CEE economies experience the effects of improved or diminished economic performance and as the efforts of their respective FDI attraction policies feed through. Perhaps more importantly, the EU Association Agreements with CEE countries will create a more stable but more regulated environment for 'footloose' investors, despite increasing competition from other emerging economies.

From a range of attractiveness/risk, three groupings can be identified within each main range of factor ratings (*Transformacja Gospodarki*, 1996; Lankes and Venables, 1996):

Legal and administrative-organisational frameworks:

- High attractiveness and low risk - Czech Republic, Hungary, Poland
- Medium attractiveness/risk - Slovenia, Slovakia, Estonia
- Low to very low attractiveness and high risk - Latvia, Moldova, Lithuania, Romania, Ukraine, Bulgaria, Russia, Belarus

Macroeconomic criteria:

- High attractiveness and low risk - Czech Republic, Poland, Slovenia, Hungary
- Medium attractiveness/risk - Estonia, Slovakia, Romania
- Low to very low attractiveness and high risk - Lithuania, Latvia, Russia, Bulgaria, Belarus, Ukraine, Moldova

Investor preference/perceived investment risk:

- Low risk and high preference - Czech Republic, Hungary
- Medium risk/preference - Poland, Slovenia, Slovakia
- Higher risk and lower preference - Estonia, Lithuania, Latvia, Romania
- Very high risk and least preferred - Russia, Belarus, Ukraine, Moldova, Bulgaria

Based upon our cumulative assessment of the various attempts to establish ratings of CEE attractiveness, incorporating objective and subjective criteria, three broad categories can be proposed. However, it must be recognised that these rankings are rather volatile and can realign dramatically as the CEE transition period works through the various obstacles to FDI attraction. They will certainly reflect any significant changes in the degree of investor confidence as CEE moves closer to both the EU and the wider international economic system:

- High overall attractiveness: Czech Republic, Hungary, Poland

- Average overall attractiveness: Slovenia, Estonia, Slovakia
- Low/poor overall attractiveness: Ukraine, Belarus, Bulgaria, Lithuania, Latvia, Russia, Romania, Moldova

In support of this league table, there are some examples of relocation to CEE. One of them is the case of Semperit relocating from Austria to the Czech Republic (Murdoch, 1997). The company decided to move out of Austria because of labour market inflexibility and high costs encountered there. However, the negative effect of this location decision was more than outweighed by Siemens' decision to locate a US$ 400 million chip plant in Villach in Austria. In the case of a chip plant, it is quality and the qualifications of workers rather that the cost of labour which mattered most, suggesting that at least in the near-future, Western European and CEE locations may appeal to different types of FDI.

In general, there appears to have been few formal attempts to estimate the future volume of inflows of foreign investment into CEE. The task is fraught with the problem of a large number of indeterminate variables, though belated but perhaps vulnerable Japanese and Korean interest has clearly altered the climate for assessing investment opportunities and the relatively high perceived investment risk by EU firms. However, again as before, it is possible to indicate potential levels by comparing CEE countries with similar economies in Western Europe. For example, it has been predicted that the Central European economies could attain the same levels of development as Spain and Portugal by 2010. FDI as a percentage of GDP in these countries has hovered between 2.2 percent and 3.8 percent in recent years (Gual and Martín, 1995). However, three of the Visegrad countries had already achieve this by 1995: Poland, 2.7 percent; Hungary, 10.7 percent; and the Czech Republic, 6.9 percent.

Consequently, annual FDI inflows to Central Europe could be between US$ 7.5 billion and 13.1 billion by 2010, compared with US$ 3.8 billion for the region as a whole in 1994, though it should be emphasised that more robust estimates of future FDI cannot be made, and membership of the EU will be key in this process.

Previous rounds of EU expansion provide some evidence with which to judge the likely effects of EU expansion to the east. In the five years after their accession to the EU, the average annual increase in the stock of extra- and intra-EU FDI into Portugal was 56.7 percent and for Spain,

128.3 percent. In the period 1990-93, the corresponding increases were 1.7 percent and 17.8 percent (Dunning, 1997). Although this may be the case in the short-term, other FDI determinants - such as market size and growth, relative factor costs and agglomeration economies - will ultimately determine FDI flows into CEE in the long-term. Competition for foreign investment from CEE is, therefore, likely to increase significantly in the short-term if these countries were to join the EU. However, this effect may turn out to be short-lived and may be limited to lower value labour-intensive assembly activities and concentrations on greenfield sites. Weak economic prospects, continuing political instability and weak legal frameworks look set to prevent a major exodus of FDI to CEE.

While overall amounts may be difficult to anticipate, other trends appear more likely to deepen. One key change in the inflow of FDI is the shift away from Hungary as the main CEE destination for foreign investment. Hungary's dominance is being challenged by Poland, where the larger economy and market as well as the positive results already achieved by the reform programme is beginning to attract the bulk of new FDI in the region. There is also an expected change in the sources of FDI, as countries such as Japan - which have hitherto had a marginal investment presence in CEE - are increasing their share of inward investment, though not on the same scale as their FDI entry into Western Europe during the 1980s. At this stage it is not possible to predict the effects which the 1997/8 economic crises in the South East Asian economies will have on their FDI commitments and strategies in CEE countries. Whatever the outcome, it is a striking example of the degree to which inward FDI investment is crucially dependent upon global factors outside of a host country's sphere of influence. This recent episode is most important as a corrective lesson when devising nationally focused economic and regional development policies, which may introduce a critical role for FDI attraction measures. Specifically, the policy process must take account of the degree to which the role of FDI in the transition process in CEE countries is subject to corporate level strategies rather than just the fulfilment national aspirations.

As well as shifts in the scale and destination of FDI, changes in the *type* of CEE investments are predicted as well. Acquisitions through the privatisation programmes should continue to encourage FDI, though in different ways in the main countries receiving investment: Hungary, the Czech Republic and Poland.

In *Hungary*, until recently, the majority of foreign investments have been based on acquisitions during the large-scale privatisations. Although privatisation will continue in public utilities - oil and gas, electricity distribution, and the remaining tranche of shares in the state telephone company - the programme is likely to attract less FDI in future as the opportunities for foreign acquirers dwindle. It has been predicted that future investment will increasingly be based on greenfield or mixed acquisition-greenfield investments, particularly in sectors supplying the major manufacturing FDI sectors in Hungary (eg. automotive components) (EIU, 1995).

One of the obstacles to FDI into the *Czech Republic* in the last few years has been the limited access of foreigners to the privatisation programme. Consequently, although the 'second wave' of privatisation is expected to start soon - with companies in a variety of sectors, including engineering, telecoms, oil refineries and chemicals - future investment into the country is likely to be drawn towards acquisitions of recently-privatised companies, joint ventures and greenfields. The latter type of investment in particular has been hindered by the process of restitution (confusing ownership and driving up the prices for undeveloped land), but this issue is being resolved (*Business Central Europe*, 1995).

Increasingly stable economic conditions in *Poland* are anticipated to encourage greenfield and joint venture investment into the country. The introduction of the long-delayed privatisation programme should also lead to a surge in FDI with the opportunities available to foreigners for acquisitions in a range of industries: pharmaceuticals, cosmetics, steel, non-ferrous metals, cars, cement, furniture, clothing, breweries, tobacco and oil refining. The most significant of these will be the sale (via floatation on the Warsaw stock exchange) of Telekomunikacja Polska during 1998 currently valued at US$ 10-15 billion (*Financial Times*, 1998).

Further, new types of FDI may emerge through 'second-generation' investments. The most important of these are extensions, 'piggy-back' investments, and 'modernisation' investments. In terms of *investment extensions*, with the successful experience of initial investments by foreign companies, some firms are expanding their presence within individual countries - such as General Motors, which is doubling the production capacity of its engine plant in Hungary. Other companies are developing independent investments in different CEE countries, such as Daewoo, which has a large automotive investment in the Czech Republic as well as a series of planned investments in the white goods sector in Poland. Further, some companies are deepening their presence in particular countries though a change in their types of investment. For example, Volvo initially entered Poland through a joint venture in an assembly plant, but in 1995, it switched to the development of a greenfield site for its own production facilities. This option has become increasingly popular among Western companies which have acquired local market knowledge through their past experiences and want to avoid conflicts of interest with joint venture partners.

The phenomenon of *'piggy-back'* investment is increasingly common in the region. Much of the investment into CEE countries has been characterised by large production projects undertaken by Western companies. The investments have often been made in industries where production relies heavily on networks of suppliers and sub-contractors, as in the automobile industry. Hence, suppliers for the Western investors may also invest in CEE markets in order to take advantage of their existing relationships and supply the new production facilities in CEE, as has already been taking place in the case of Volkswagen's acquisition of Skoda.

Modernisation programmes underway in some CEE countries should create new opportunities for Western firms to invest in CEE markets. For example, the substantial investments in improving the telecommunications infrastructure in some CEE countries should create opportunities for more sophisticated, service providers to establish a presence.

Lastly, a significant economic transition issue facing all the CEE countries is how to attract FDI which will add value to both economic *and* institutional rebuilding efforts. In this respect, there is an example of high value-added greenfield site development which became apparent in Silicon Valley in California, and Silicon Glen in Central Scotland. These FDI programmes targeted centres of excellence in manufacturing capacity, including firms and their workforces. However, the crucial element in terms of the region's attractiveness was its institutional framework, predominantly the locality's universities and other further education colleges, and government support for R&D-based FDI. A similar pattern could emerge in CEE countries as the competition for FDI within an enlarged EU shifts away from transient labour cost advantages, to more stable higher-value activities. The initial signs of this potential for CEE countries are already apparent but need further research in order to determine its longer term viability. The positive signals come from both Gyor in Hungary and Krakow in Poland. A good example is the recent FDI move by Motorola (US). It has announced a US $ 150 million investment in Krakow with an anticipated 500 person workforce, of which up to one third could be Ph.D graduates. This project will be a 67 ha. development based close to the Jagellonian University campus, and attract SEZ status for 12 years. The SEZ will also encompass the scientific and research resources available within southern Poland. The key feature is an educational-industrial network comprising the University, Polytechnic, Local Council, Sendzimir Steel Mill, and the national Treasury. This network of institutions will offer both scientific and research collaboration, and substantial staff training facilities (*Rzeczpopolita*, 1998).

Conclusions

Future foreign investment into the region will depend principally on the ability of the CEE countries to establish stable economic and political environments with a regulatory climate favourable to foreign investors. In addition, the rise in market demand, continuing labour cost advantages and recognition of CEE advantages in other production factors (such as skilled labour) are likely to maintain FDI increases to the region in future. The emerging role of CEE policy on FDI should also have an impact, especially as CEE inward investment agencies begin to market CEE locations more actively.

As competition for inward investment intensifies in CEE and comparative advantages change along with global patterns of investment opportunities, it is crucial that policy-makers have a clear understanding of what they wish to achieve by their efforts to attract FDI. There are several dimensions to this important issue of the clarity of FDI attraction policy objectives.

The first concerns the anticipated role and perceived benefits of FDI in the context of transition, and equally important in the longer term as CEE becomes more integrated into an enlarged EU. These elements of policy comprise key aspects of both macro- and meso-levels of analysis which are intended to raise economic performance and enhance the means by which this can be achieved. Broadly speaking, they can be identified in most CEE countries as:

- active participation of FDI in the privatisation process, which can not be sustained by domestic capital (UNCTAD, 1994);
- capital inflow avoiding indebtedness for economic development, assisting monetary and fiscal policy;
- technology transfer (hard and soft) more directly through *in situ* involvement in production, skill transference and spin-off effects; and
- increased export performance to new markets (and market share) accompanying relocated subsidiaries and greenfield developments, and potential import substitution effects.

Second, a frequently overlooked feature of inward investment concerns the relative merits of the method and mode it adopts, and thus which of these should FDI attraction policy target or support (Blomstrom and Kokko, 1997). Key economic policy objectives at national and regional levels can be linked to the form which FDI takes, such as portfolio, acquisition, joint ventures and greenfield site. An understanding of FDI impact on local economies is particularly important with respect to its positive and negative effects on local producers - supplier network participation or displacement by existing foreign suppliers following FDI, and competition on grounds of quality and productivity requirements.

Third, there is the very basic matter of the cost of attraction policies, and the expected gains from both financial and fiscal measures. This is well illustrated by the positions adopted by two of the most recently established, independent CEE states: the Czech and Slovak Republics. The *Czech Republic* has been highly successful in attracting FDI, regarding its comparative advantages as sufficiently attractive without the need to resort to significant tangible incentives until 1998; however, it does have in place an extremely professional and successful inward investment agency. In contrast, the *Slovak Republic,* though well regarded, has had little success in attracting FDI; although it recently won a major investment project by

Sony for a component manufacturing facility against Czech competition. It does not have a coherent pro-active attraction policy, lacks consistent advocacy from senior government officials with regards to FDI and privatisation, and with few state resources available for inward investment promotion cannot radically alter Slovakia's competitive position. For example, the national inward investment agency is predominantly self-financing (an unusual feature among CEE inward investment agencies) with partial support from EU/Phare funding.

The cost and effectiveness measures applied to attraction policies and implementation by various inward investment promotion agencies are difficult to establish. However, a recent evaluation by the European Commission of all Phare and UK Know-How Fund-supported CEE foreign investment agencies (except Latvia), reported that there had been a sharp improvement in the quality of inward investment support, and international trade and investment performance (CEC, 1997a). This evaluation also confirmed that it is not possible yet to link specific investments to the output of these agencies given the timespan of the investment process and intervening factors.

At a national level, GDP spend on any incentives, and inward investment location agencies, reduces funds available to regions, local authorities, and general infrastructure programmes. Competitive pressures to improve attractiveness will vary according to both the adequacy of existing institutional and infrastructural conditions, and the degree to which countries can actually afford to plough scarce resources into FDI bidding contests. However, it seems clear that transition phase advantages for the major players in CEE will be relatively short lived and that fine-tuning policy objectives or failing to invest in attraction measures could impair FDI opportunities. Attempting to entice and let in all investors is a policy position which is difficult to resist under current conditions. Competition between CEE economies will intensify as each country better equips itself for FDI bids and tries to conjoin the contribution of inward investment with longer term development goals. Therefore, short-term cost factors are unlikely to deter policy competition except in extreme cases where very small and peripheral economies simply cannot afford to develop a sustainable range of state-funded incentives or institutional support. Within a local context, the impact is difficult to predict but potentially there is a substantial effect on revenues foregone from locally-negotiated incentives (eg. in Poland, the local tax office has jurisdiction).

Fourth, an important issue to be incorporated into any FDI attraction policy is the effect of an EU Association Agreement on competition between CEE countries for inward investment. This will include rivalry between CEE and Western European countries, within and outside the EU, and between regions within CEE. Due to the signing of each Association Agreement by individual CEE countries, potential investors also start to weigh up the pros and cons of either locating in the EU for future export to CEE or producing in CEE for export to the EU.

It is also apparent that CEE economies are competing with the established and rapidly developing countries of South-East Asia and Latin America (*Rzeczpospolita*, 1997). Thus, location advantages are likely to continue to shift as both global and, more obviously, EU economic and political factors inform corporate strategy rather than follow policy-makers' 'wish-lists'. On the other hand, looking at the experiences of Spain and Portugal, it is quite clear that as soon as the CEE countries entered a period of negotiation for EU membership they became more attractive to foreign investors.

Finally, specific and targeted incentives tend not to work in conditions where there are major infrastructure problems. These measures simply cannot compensate for the inhibiting factors which corporate decision-takers experience when evaluating potential investment options. This is well illustrated with regards to the effects of taxation regimes. Therefore, since most FDI is directed towards manufacturing (predominantly low-skill/low-wage assembly work) or tertiary sector development (professional services, retailing and trading firms), it would seem appropriate to channel any funds or policy effort to these areas and de-link this from future hopes of privatisation initiatives as these will recede in terms of FDI attractiveness.

If future FDI promotion policy in CEE is to be at all successful, it must confront additional issues with regards to their social as well as economic and geo-political advantage over competitors within an enlarged EU. From recent research into location strategy, it is important for CEE inward investment agencies and their governing policy frameworks to strengthen linkages with local authorities in a concerted and well-planned approach to FDI 'bidding' (Hughes and Helinska-Hughes, 1997).

Particularly interesting in this regard is the degree to which investment in CEE and EU enlargement is producing transnational communities, expressing demands for additional social infrastructure on top of economic/physical improvements. In this sense, FDI attraction policy should focus upon the positive side of promotion at more local levels where industrial networks and communities develop, especially with regards to the substantial benefits which can be gained from encouraging greenfield site investment projects within designated zones.

Table 3.2 Financial incentives in selected CEE countries

	Hungary	Poland	Czech Republic	Slovak Republic	Slovenia
Investment size	i) Min. 15 mn HUF [1,2] ii) Min. 10 bn HUF iii) Min. 1 bn HUF in dev. areas iv) Min. 3 bn HUF in dev. areas	i) Min. 50 MECU [3] ii) SEZs	Min. US$ 25 mn in manufact.	DM 1 mn since 31.12.92	none
Minimum foreign holding (%)	i) 30 ii) -iv) none	i) - ii) none	none	30	none
Tax-free years	i) - ii) 10 iii) 5 iv) 10	i) none ii) 10	5	2 years [5]	none
Further tax concessions and reduced rates	i) 1st 5 yrs at 100%; 2nd 5 yrs at 40% ii) until 2001 at 100% iii) 50% iv) until 2008 at 100%	i) no limit, with partial exemption[4] ii) next 10 yrs at 50%	Tax credits	none	Up to 40% reduced tax base under some conditions
Other incentives	i) - iv) A	i) B	C	C	D
Customs incentives	Yes	Yes	Yes	Yes	Yes

Source: Stankovsky (1995), supplemented by authors' data for 1997.

Notes to Table 3.2
[1] Production sector enterprises
[2] If criteria met before 31 December 1993
[3] For enterprises locating in underdeveloped regions or introducing new technologies
[4] Not to exceed the transaction value or the equity holding of the foreign investor
[5] For profits only.

Key to Table 3.2: Other incentives for foreign direct investment in CEE

A   Reduced-rate tax if reinvesting profit from 1993; losses can be carried forward
    for up to five years, or indefinitely in some cases; and dividends transferred
    abroad are not taxed at source.
B   Three years' losses can be carried forward in equal amounts; since 15 February
    1992, losses can be offset against future earnings; and the financial year does
    not have to be calendar year.
C   Losses can be carried forward up to seven years from 1992 in the Czech
    Republic, and for share and investment funds losses after 1996; tax relief and
    other incentives do not apply to acquisitions; tax incentives for investment in
    Eastern Slovakia; and zero duty on imported machinery.
D   Other tax incentives for companies operating in free trade areas, less-developed
    or sparsely-populated areas; and reinvesting profits reduces tax liability by up
    to 15 percent.

Part II:
Policy Competition

4 Financial Incentives

PHILIP RAINES

Introduction

Of the different policy areas discussed in this study, the one most closely associated with the attraction of foreign investment in Europe is financial incentives, especially regional grants for capital investment. Over the past decade, the majority of large, mobile foreign investment projects in Western Europe - and increasingly in Central and Eastern Europe - have been linked to the offer of regional financial incentive packages by national and local authorities. In Ireland, for example, in the late 1980s, nearly 80 percent of all greenfield investments by foreign firms received financial assistance.

Financial incentives can include a range of policy instruments, including tax concessions and employment subsidies, but by far the most common form of incentive is capital grants to industry to influence location in specially-designated areas. Grant assistance is available in all Western European countries apart from Denmark, which offers no formal alternative, and is the core of all regional incentive systems, apart from Greece. In the Netherlands, Spain and the UK - countries with active FDI promotion policies - capital grants are the only regional financial incentive offered for nearly all eligible areas (Yuill, Bachtler and Wishlade, 1996).

Financial incentives are the principal policy instrument for regional policy in Western Europe, reflecting how foreign investment has become closely linked with regional economic development. As noted in Chapter 2, attracting FDI to less-prosperous regions has become a common objective in many European countries, mainly because large, mobile investment projects tend to involve significant job creation. With the surge of foreign investment into the Community during the 1980s and 1990s, regional policy-makers increasingly made the attraction of foreign investment a key goal in regional policy, though it has rarely been pursued to the exclusion of other policy approaches, such as direct support for indigenous business. Indeed, FDI promotion has been viewed in tandem with the development of local industry, as incoming foreign plants can result in the transfer of new technologies, production methods and training to local businesses, and the different policy approaches have been seen as complementing each other (Brown, 1996).

As the potential value of FDI has risen in the estimation of regional policy-makers, the use of regional incentives to attract foreign investment projects has been increasing. In a survey for its review of global FDI trends, UNCTAD (1995) noted that a larger range of incentives are being used by a greater number of countries than a decade ago. Although their growth has been contained within the EU by European Commission competition regulations on State aids (as discussed more fully in the following chapter), regional incentives continue to account for large shares of public sector expenditure on regional economic development. Even where financial incentives have been declining in expenditure terms, their link to FDI attraction remains strong. For example, in Great Britain, despite the fact that relatively few regional incentive awards have been made to FDI projects (representing less than ten percent of the total number of awards between 1984 and 1995), they have accounted for between approximately 45 and 55 percent of the value of all Regional Selective Assistance offers (Industrial Development Act 1982, various years).

Against this background, the following chapter examines the issues from a number of perspectives. First, it considers the theoretical underpinnings of the use of regional incentives in attracting foreign investment projects, and the extent to which this has influenced policy design. Second, it reviews the evidence in Western Europe for regional incentives influencing location decisions. Lastly, the chapter assesses whether the use of regional incentives in FDI promotion has resulted in greater policy competition among Western European governments, looking at changes in award rates, spatial coverage and overall expenditure over time.

Location Decisions and the Use of Incentives

In Western Europe, grants in general, and capital grants in particular, are the mainstay of almost all the regional incentive packages on offer. Indeed, only Greece does not have a regional incentive package which is strongly capital-grant-oriented - here, applicant firms have a choice between alternative fiscal and financial aid packages, with a current emphasis on the *fiscal* incentives on offer, reflecting *inter alia* past problems in Greece with the effective administration and funding of financial incentives. Elsewhere, countries have capital grants as the most prominent component of their regional incentive packages. In contrast to the high profile attached to capital grants in most regional incentive packages, regional loan-related support is prominent in just six countries: Austria, Flanders in Belgium, Germany, Greece, Portugal and Northern Ireland in the UK. Moreover, nowhere are loan-related subsidies a major component of the regional incentive package. For example, the ERP Regional Loan in Germany is available only to projects which do *not* have a 'primary effect' (ie. which are *not* regionally-exporting) and, therefore, which do *not* qualify for the main German regional incentive, the Investment Grant.

The reliance on grants in Western Europe distinguishes it from other parts of the world, where loan support and fiscal incentives are more common (UNCTAD, 1995). This reasons for this are not wholly clear, in that those cited by European policy-makers do not appear to be unique the region's historical and present economic and policy circumstances. The arguments in favour of capital grants within regional incentive packages are numerous (Allen, Hull and Yuill, 1979): from the perspective of the aid applicant, they are generally both highly visible and easy to understand; from the viewpoint of the policy-maker they are straightforward to administer and yet afford considerable flexibility; and, as far as the EU Competition Policy Directorate is concerned, they are the simplest of incentive types to police, falling readily within the Commission's net grant equivalent aid valuation methodology and ceilings.

In contrast, loan-related measures are not always attractive to applicants, at least in the EU (especially those which are already highly geared or have easy access to sources of finance), and carry with them far greater administrative burdens than grants. This reflects the fact that greater sums of public money tend to be 'at risk' (ie. the loan principal as well as the subsidy component of any award) and that project monitoring is usually of longer duration (related to the pay-back period of the loan). As a consequence, over the past decade there has been a notable reduction in the degree to which loan-related support has been available within the regional financial assistance packages of Western European and a corresponding increased stress on grant-related assistance.

Regional incentive grants are used by governments to compensate for a region's relative absence of certain locational advantages, as translated into the perceived additional costs to a company in locating there. In traditional location theory, foreign investment decisions are made through comparing a series of short- and long-term costs among several locations (CEC, 1993; Dunning, 1993). These costs differ depending on the nature of the activity being placed - production, distribution or administrative facilities, in manufacturing or service sectors - but can be considered in terms of the following categories:

- *establishment costs*: those involved in the initial setting up or expansion of a facility - including the availability of an appropriate site and the costs of its development and construction - and any costs incurred in bringing the facility up to its anticipated operational strength;

- *operating costs*: those associated with the normal running of the facility, including the relative costs of labour at different skills levels and capital equipment purchase and maintenance, as well as the costs of acquiring local external inputs and services, ensuring local suppliers can provide at adequate quality levels or importing the necessary inputs and services from outside the region;

- *market costs*: those arising from accessing target markets, such as distribution and market development; and

- *development costs*: those determining the scope allowed by the investment for expanding production, entering new geographical markets and developing new products.

From the perspective of traditional FDI promotion, regional financial incentives only directly affect one of the location factor categories noted above: *establishment* costs. These costs can be lowered through the provision of financial support for greenfields and site expansions. As they tend to take the form of one-off or short-term payments, their influence on investment decisions would appear to be greater in projects where the establishment and expansion costs are relatively high compared to longer-term costs (operating, market and development). As establishment costs remain a significant consideration in many investment projects, financial incentives can be a key instrument in inward investment policy for affecting decisions.

Nevertheless, regional incentives are not specifically aimed at foreign investment, but at generating additional investment in less-developed regions regardless of its origin. In general, they have not been explicitly or exclusively designed to attract FDI projects, although in some countries (notably the UK) it is arguable that major regional grants would have been abolished if they were not needed to compete for FDI. The only incentive scheme in Western Europe that openly aims to influence international FDI location is the capital grant in Northern Ireland (in the UK), which offers a discretionary award of up to 20 percent on top of the normal capital support grant for desirable internationally-mobile projects. What has allowed incentives to be used increasingly for FDI promotion has been the fact that the characteristics of FDI projects tend to be favoured by what were originally designed as neutral criteria. This can be seen in the following aspects of incentive schemes, influencing both the eligibility and values of incentives awards: a project's eligible activities; its type; its size; and awareness of international competition for its attraction.

With respect to the *eligible activities* of regional incentives, there are broad similarities in the approach of different schemes between European countries. The emphasis has been on eligibility criteria that tend to benefit foreign investments - especially projects which have an international locational choice - since policies are generally oriented towards activities that are mobile and do not serve only local markets. With all incentives, the intention is to avoid supporting local services that might displace existing jobs within the region. In Germany, Investment Grant assistance is restricted to projects that have a 'primary effect', that is, those that export most of the goods and services outside the region (the region here being precisely defined in spatial terms). Although no other country apart from Germany has so carefully specified the primary effect, similar principles are applied elsewhere, often involving restrictions on the scope of eligible economic activities. Hence, in the Netherlands, the Investment Premium is limited to projects whose economic activities can be described as 'footloose' (ie. they have a choice of location and an impact outside the local market).

Project-type criteria applied to incentives also tend to benefit FDI. In attracting foreign investment projects, the focus is mainly on capturing large, mobile projects that will become new establishments in the target region. This objective can be seen in the emphasis in regional incentives on setting-up projects, which are often supported over other project types - such as expansion or acquisitions - because they usually involve greater job creation (and are more likely to be considered mobile). Consequently, in France, setting-up projects have lower job creation ceilings in order to become eligible for assistance from *prime d'aménagement du territoire* (or PAT).

With regard to *project size*, regional incentives can indirectly favour FDI projects because of their preference for large projects. As mobile foreign investment projects are usually large, incentives can influence both eligibility criteria and award values. In terms of the eligibility criteria, few countries operate explicit limits in their schemes, apart from Spain and France, which have minimum size thresholds. Even in countries without explicit limits, size - and, in particular, the level of job creation - is influential in determining the rate of award. In the Netherlands, for example, the number of jobs created influences the value of discretionary awards made to large projects. In Italy, although there is no discretion under the existing system, job creation is one of three key factors determining the case for support.

Lastly, *international competition* for projects may lead policy-makers to consider what level of assistance will be necessary to bring the project to their country. In Spain, for example, the rate of award calculated from applying the internal formula is always well below the published ceiling. Yet if the project is of particular interest, and especially if there are known to be other countries competing for the investment, the indicative offer may be raised. This can also take place in the UK by application of the so-called 'additionality' criterion under Regional Selective Assistance, which means that the level of support can be raised to the minimum necessary to enable a project to proceed or be attracted to a UK location.

In practice, even where influencing international locational choice is not directly mentioned, FDI projects are still favoured under the main regional incentive schemes. This is evident in the case of Great Britain from a comparison of trends in foreign investment and domestic project awards over time (Table 4.1). Although fewer incentive offers have been made for FDI projects, as a whole, they have generated a larger volume of associated investment than domestic projects. Not surprisingly, on average, FDI projects have received consistently higher award rates than domestic projects, suggesting that FDI projects appear to be preferred in the use of regional incentives in practice even if not in principle. This is also reflected in the greater significance of the average foreign investment project. Not only has the investment associated with the average FDI project been larger than for the average domestic project, but it has been increasing over time - between 1984-86 and 1993-95, the associated investment with average FDI projects increased from £6.7 million to £8.4 million, whereas for domestic projects, it stayed constant at £0.8 million (representing a decline in real terms).

For some countries, the aim of using regional incentive schemes is not principally attracting foreign investment, but retaining mobile domestic investment. As noted in Chapter 2, German authorities have been interested more in halting domestic investment flight - as a result of the country's relatively high labour costs, taxation levels and perception of restrictive employment legislation - rather than attracting new investment, so the focus of incentive usage is on supporting domestic investment expansions rather than influencing greenfield decisions.

The Impact of Incentives on Location Decisions

The evidence for the effectiveness of regional incentives in attracting foreign investment is mixed. Individual company data on the importance of regional incentives tend to be lacking, as there are few case studies of investment decisions involving regional incentives, owing to the confidentiality of the transactions. In most cases, official information is not even available on the value of awards offered to specific companies. Nevertheless, numerous business surveys have been conducted of investors about the relevance of incentives in their investment decisions and for the most part, the studies have shown that incentives tend not to be the key location factor - at least in terms of the *country* of location - and remain subsidiary to other determinants (eg. Bachtler and Clement, 1990a;

PACEC, 1989). For example, a survey by Ernst & Young of 67 manufacturing investments revealed financial assistance to have been less critical or important in decisions about the country of investment than the following factors: proximity to markets; availability of raw materials and components; general availability of labour; cost of labour; and the quality of road and rail services (CEC, 1993).

Table 4.1 GB Regional Selective Assistance offers, 1984-1995

	FDI projects			
	No. of offers	Value of offers (£m)	Associated investment (£m)	Average award rate (%)
1984-86	430	293.9	2,884.0	9.8
1987-89	287	299.1	3,371.4	11.3
1990-92	297	342.4	2,820.9	8.2
1993-95	424	399.7	3,542.3	8.9
	Domestic projects			
	No. of offers	Value of offers (£m)	Associated investment (£m)	Average award rate (%)
1984-86	2,324	245.4	1,831.5	7.5
1987-89	4,253	309.7	3,270.9	10.6
1990-92	3,494	475.9	3,811.9	8.0
1993-95	3,670	477.2	3,082.4	6.5

Source: Industrial Development Act 1982 (various years).

The relatively low ranking accorded to financial incentives in surveys needs to be interpreted carefully. Financial incentives may be crucial in determining where within a country a firm invests, either regionally or at site level. Econometric research analysing FDI patterns in the UK shows that along with other cost-related factors, financial incentives do play an important factor in securing projects at the regional level (Hill and Munday, 1995). Another study of incoming FDI in the UK during the period 1984-91 also found that financial incentives were significant in determining the spatial distribution of FDI, with most Japanese companies locating in UK assisted areas (Taylor, 1993). Owing to the fact that the location criteria for any given project will vary depending on the qualitative nature of the investment project, the importance of financial incentives in determining FDI locational patterns is clearly not constant. Christodoulou (1996) claims that financial incentives can assume critical significance for: projects where two or three locations are identified as meeting the key criteria for the project; and for high technology capital-intensive projects. In particular examples, regional incentives have been frequently highlighted as decisive in the selection of particular regions, though in practice it is difficult to identify these cases because of the commercial and political sensitivity involved in regional incentive payments and inward investment negotiations. In the Ernst & Young survey, it was noted that incentives were considered critical or important in the choice of region for 60 percent of manufacturing investments in Spain and 40 percent in the UK (CEC, 1993). Begg and McDowell (1986) concluded that regional incentives had influenced project location by foreign companies in the UK, and similar conclusions were reached in smaller studies of investment in Northern Ireland (Sheehan, 1993) and Wales (Hill and Munday, 1995).

In most major foreign investment decisions (especially greenfield cases), the process of determining a location produces a range of suitable sites. While these sites may be chosen on the basis of the cost factors identified above, in Western Europe, several locations can satisfy the key criteria. For example, in many industries, 'market proximity' refers to a site that can serve a Europe-wide market rather than a geographically-specific customer (as in the case of components suppliers locating near particular assembly plants); 'labour skills' can mean the availability of workers with general engineering skills and not special technical knowledge, and so on. What investors consider the most important locational factors is not necessarily what is the *determining* factor in practice. Hence, the final selection of site has often depended largely on the financial package offered by the region or country. Incentives are used to bolster rather than compensate for existing location determinants, but that does not diminish their importance in competition with sites possessing the same location advantages. Although companies tend to play down the role of incentives in investment decisions - which may be in their interests in order to affirm their that their commitment to a certain location will extend beyond the period grant payments - research has shown that they can be effective when such a 'shortlist' of potential sites has been formed, as appears to be the norm (Bachtler and Clement, 1990b).

Indeed, for some investments - especially those where the range of suitable locations was wide and the investment establishment costs were relatively high - companies used a map of assisted areas as a method of shortlisting location early in the site selection procedure. The final investment decision might eventually be based on non-incentive factors - reversing the usual hierarchy for prioritising location factors - but companies can be interested in retaining the option of a grant offer before close examination of potential sites.

Similarly, no definitive picture of the impact of incentives emerges when looking at links between the distribution of regional incentive spending and foreign investment by region. In theory, it would be expected that regions of high incentive expenditure would have a relatively high share of foreign investment. Again, there is a problem with establishing a counterfactual, but given that areas where regional incentives are available tend to have limited investment advantages, it might be anticipated that incentives would at least allow for a relatively more level distribution of FDI.

However, when examining regional incentive expenditure and the regional distribution of total foreign investment (in countries for which comparative data is available), a close connection appears in some countries but not in others. Hill and Munday (1995) argued that a significant positive association existed between incentive expenditure and the share of projects and FDI-related jobs of particular regions in France and the UK between 1980 and 1990. In the case of France, this conclusion is reinforced by evidence from the period 1990 and 1993, as the two regions winning the highest shares of FDI also had the highest levels of regional incentive spending - Nord-Pas-de-Calais and Lorraine accounted for 27 percent of new FDI employment and 36.6 percent of grant expenditure (Wishlade *et al*, 1996).

In contrast, the influence of regional grants on foreign investment is difficult to establish in the case of Spain, Italy and Germany. Between 1987 and 1991, in Spain, two-thirds of total foreign investment was located in the Madrid and Catalonia regions where regional grants were not available; in contrast, nearly a third of incentive spending in the same period was in Murcia, which only accounted for 0.3 percent of new FDI (Mella Márquez, 1994; Wishlade *et al*, 1996). Similarly, in Italy, by 1994, the largest share of employment in foreign-controlled companies was in

Lombardy (53.7 percent) and Piemonte (12.2 percent), though investments in neither region were eligible for grants (Cominotti and Mariotti, 1994; Wishlade *et al*, 1996). Over half of new West German FDI between 1990 and 1993 was located in the *Länder* of Bayern and Baden-Württemburg, but only locations in Bayern were eligible for regional financial assistance. Nearly 60 percent of regional incentive spending was in North-Rhine Westphalia and Lower Saxony, but they accounted for less than a quarter of new FDI flows (Wishlade *et al*, 1996).

A more detailed picture can be presented in the case of manufacturing by comparing regional incentive expenditure and foreign-owned manufacturing employment in Great Britain (Table 4.2). Between 1986 and 1991, employment in foreign-owned manufacturing rose quicker in assisted areas (30.5 percent) than non-assisted areas (19.2 percent growth), lifting the share of the assisted areas in total foreign-owned employment from 38.6 to 42.4 percent (CSO, various years). This would indicate that there may be a link between the use of regional incentives and foreign investment attraction, but an analysis of employment change showed that foreign-owned employment grew faster in the assisted than the non-assisted areas in only three of the eight regions. In the regions receiving the highest shares of expenditure - Wales and Scotland - foreign-owned employment growth rates in the assisted areas were either equivalent to the non-assisted areas (Wales) or considerably smaller (Scotland). Over half of the offers were made in these two regions, but their share of total employment growth was only just over a fifth. In contrast, the North and the West Midlands accounted for over half of the new employment in the assisted areas, but only received a quarter of the expenditure.

Even when examining all manufacturing employment change, the impact of regional incentives is unclear. Manufacturing employment as a whole declined in Great Britain during this period. Only half of the country's regions had assisted areas whose rate of decline was less than non-assisted areas or who registered overall growth, suggesting that the impact of incentives in changing the relative rates of decline was weak.

While incentive expenditure may have been influential in FDI attraction in some regions, other factors appear to have been greater determinants. A simple comparison of employment growth in assisted and non-assisted areas does not allow for consideration of the range of factors affecting changes in local labour markets. It may be that regional incentive spending has compensated for weaknesses in the assisted areas and prevented larger gaps from appearing between the growth of foreign-owned employment in non-assisted and assisted areas. However, the correspondence between the shares in regional incentive spending and the growth of foreign-owned employment between 1986 and 1991 does not provide strong support for incentives as a determining factor. The overall net growth in foreign-owned employment in the assisted regions may be partly linked to the sluggish growth in foreign-owned employment in the South East, possibly reflecting a migration of some foreign-owned companies from the higher cost region.

Table 4.2 Manufacturing employment and incentive spending by GB region, 1986-91

	Non-assisted areas		Assisted areas			
	(% change)		*(% change)*		% all new foreign-owned employ-ment	% total incentive offer value
	Foreign-owned employ-ment	All employ-ment	Foreign-owned employ-ment	All employ-ment		
E. Anglia	-1.9	-2.4	-	-	-	-
E. Midlands	67.6	-4.8	40.9	7.8	1.2	0.4
North	21.7	-7.0	43.7	-3.7	17.2	14.1
North West	42.5	-6.6	10.8	-9.7	9.4	11.9
Scotland	40.8	-0.8	10.8	-9.6	7.7	31.0
South East	4.0	-16.2	-	-	-	-
South West	23.9	-5.3	-2.6	-5.5	-0.3	2.3
Wales	24.2	-9.9	25.0	8.3	12.4	23.2
W. Midlands	74.8	-0.1	78.5	-2.8	37.8	10.8
Yorks./ Humber.	70.1	-4.5	66.7	-1.9	14.5	5.2
Great Britain	19.2	-9.4	30.5	-4.0	100.0	100.0

Source: CSO, Industrial Development Act 1982 (various years).

Ultimately, the combination of the limited availability of information and the unique characteristics of each investment decisions (making case studies essential) render it almost impossible to assess adequately the effectiveness of incentives. Although clear cost limits are operated by individual governments, the methodological problems involved in forming counterfactuals (ie. what would have happened if the investor had *not* received a grant and what would have happened if the investment had *not* been made) have weakened most efforts at cost-benefit analyses. As a result, the *net* value of FDI projects - placing direct and indirect job, income and competitive gains against the costs to the public purse and the negative effects of investors on local economies - has tended to be assumed rather than verified by most governments. This uncertainty has not only allowed policy-makers scope for using incentives, but may have encouraged competition between governments in attracting FDI projects.

Incentives and Policy Competition

The increasing association of large investment location decisions with financial incentive packages has led to concerns being expressed that rather than allowing less-favoured regions to compete more effectively for foreign investment, regional incentives often represent a costly means of attracting foreign investment (UNCTAD, 1995; Amin and Tomaney, 1995). It has been suggested that a process of competitive outbidding may be taking place between countries, as inward investment agencies feel pressure to offer larger grants to companies than their rivals. As a common feature of inward investment promotion in the US - where bidding between states appears to have driven up the value of grant offers - it has been argued that it should be less evident in Western Europe, especially in the EU, where regulatory controls are in place to prevent this (as described more fully in the next chapter). Nevertheless, the scope for competitive bidding has been increasing in Western Europe. The number of agencies specifically established for the purpose of promoting inward investment has proliferated in recent years, with new national agencies established in countries such as Denmark, Finland, Greece and Sweden and existing agencies expanding their network of representative offices and becoming autonomous organisations rather than subsidiary parts of government ministries (as has taken place in France). Furthermore, in pursuing foreign investment promotion, competition between agencies appears to have risen substantially. Anecdotal evidence abounds of companies being bombarded by inquiries from inward investment agencies when announcements of the intention to locate new projects are made (*Corporate Location*, 1996c). At national level, there has been concern that the often-intense rivalry between regional agencies can be counterproductive in a national perspective - for example, in the UK, it has been suggested within the Treasury that inward investment policy should be centralised to avoid competition between Welsh, Scottish and national inward promotion agencies (*The Economist*, 1996a).

Measuring the effects of policy competition is very difficult for a number of reasons. Governments and inward investment agencies are usually very reluctant to release grant information because of commercial confidentiality. Where information is publicly available, distinctions between incentive offers relating to domestic and foreign investments are often not made. Nevertheless, to ascertain whether competition is taking place in using incentives to attract FDI, a number of crude measures can be used to indicate - at least in broad terms - whether policy competition is occurring. The most revealing of these 'tests' are:

- *award rates*: as when these have been rising faster than inflation or in one country relative to other European countries;
- *spatial coverage*: as countries have been extending their spatial coverage for incentive usage in order to maximise their chances of securing projects; and
- *incentive expenditure*: as countries increase their overall spending on regional incentives relative to their neighbours, potentially suggesting an increased determination to secure projects.

Award Rates

Award rates in Western Europe are limited by aid ceilings - which set maxima for the percentage of an investment project's eligible expenditure that can be met by incentive awards. Award rates depend not only on the geographical location within a country but also the type of project under consideration (Table 4.3). Countries such as Greece, Ireland, Portugal and Spain are allowed high maximum levels of award (up to 75 percent of eligible investment), because of their relatively low levels of prosperity. Low ceilings are applied in more prosperous countries: Germany (especially the western *Länder*), Belgium and the Netherlands.

Table 4.3 Maximum award rates [1] (% of project capital expenditure)

Country	Designated Problem Region	Maximum Grant Award (%)[2]
Austria	Designated Areas	15-40 nge
Belgium[3]	Zones 1 and 2	20 and 15 nge
Denmark[4]	Priority Regions	25
Finland	Development Area 1	37
	Development Area 2	35
	Development Area 3	20
France	Maximum Zones	25
	Standard Zones	17
Germany[5]	GA Areas	18/15/12/10
	East Germany	23/20/15
Greece[6]	Thrace	45-55
	Other Region D	35-45
	Region C	25-40
	Region B	15-40
	Region A	0-40
Ireland[7]	Designated Areas	60
	Non-Designated	45
Italy[8]	*Mezzogiorno* A	65/50 nge
	Mezzogiorno B	55/40 nge
	Mezzogiorno C	40/25 nge
	Centre-North	20/10 nge
Luxembourg[9]	Designated Areas	25/20/17.5
Netherlands[10]	IPR Areas	20
Norway	Designated Areas	25-50 nge
Portugal	Development Areas	75
Spain	Zone 1	50-75
	Zone 2	40-45
	Zone 3	30
	Zone 4	0-20
Sweden	Development Area 1	40
	Development Area 2	35
	Temporary Areas	20
Switzerland	Designated Areas	50
UK	Northern Ireland	50
	Development Areas	30 nge
	Intermediate Areas	20 nge

Source: Compiled from Yuill, Bachtler and Wishlade (1996)

Notes for Table 4.3: [1] For some countries the maxima are set in gross terms; for others, the figures are net grant equivalents (or 'nge') - this refers to the actual value of the grant after tax. [2] These are the advertised ceilings under the main regional aid grant schemes. [3] Under the federal system in Belgium, regional policy is the responsibility of the regional governments of Flanders and Wallonia. The average award figures are for 1992-94. [4] There is no regional aid programme operating. Awards would only be considered in the context of a potential major mobile investment project. [5] The average award figure for Germany relates to the period 1991-93. [6] The average award figure relates to 1988. [7] The average award figure relates to 1990. [8] The average award figure relates to 1996. [9] The average award figure relates to the period 1992-94. [10] The average award figure relates to the period 1993-95.

Maximum rate ceilings give an indication of the potential for giving relatively high grant awards, but in practice, incentive offers tend to be well within the ceilings. When examining average award rates, the highest offers have been made in countries as diverse as Greece, Ireland, Italy, Sweden, Portugal and Northern Ireland within the UK, whereas low rates have prevailed in France, the Netherlands and western Germany.

Within these limits, average award rates do not appear to have been driven up by competition for foreign investment. Although comparative figures for awards to FDI projects are not available in Western Europe, overall rates for all awards in the main incentive schemes averaged across periods can be used as a useful proxy. When examined, the statistics suggest that average award rates have *declined* rather than risen (Table 4.4). Only Germany and the UK have witnessed rising average award rates, and in the case of Germany, the jump between the 1988-90 and 1991-93 periods largely reflects the inclusion of Germany's eastern *Länder* in regional policy (in the western *Länder*, rates have continued to fall). The link with investment flows would seem tenuous, given that the two countries are at opposite ends of the spectrum in terms of their attractiveness to new FDI. Similarly, steady falls in average award rates have occurred in France and the Netherlands, but this does not appear to have affected their ability to attract foreign investment relative to other Western European countries (especially in France, where FDI flows have surged in recent years).

Table 4.4 Average award rates (% of project capital expenditure)

Country[1]	1984-87	1988-91	1992-95
Belgium:[2]			
- Flanders	17.2	10.5	11.5
- Wallonia	15.5	13.5	13.8
France	13.3	7.1	5.8
Germany[3]	8.7	7.5	16.4
Ireland[4]	30.1	26.5	-
Italy[4]	35.6	32.8	-
Luxembourg[3]	15.7	17.8	15.3
Netherlands[5]	14.6	11.1	10.0
Portugal[6]	-	28.7	27.5
Spain[7]	16.4	24.0	15.6
Sweden	27.7	24.7	27.5
UK:			
- Great Britain	9.2	11.2	13.2
- Northern Ireland[8]	-	26.0	26.2

Source: Yuill, Bachtler and Wishlade, 1996.
Notes: [1] Greece has not been included as information is not available after 1988. [2] Figures are presented for the 1992-94 period. Note that Flanders is considered separately from Wallonia because different incentive schemes operate in each area. [3] Figures are presented for the periods 1988-90 and 1991-93 as these reflect the period before and after the inclusion of Germany's eastern *Länder* in the regional incentive system. [4] Figures are not available for the 1992-95 period. [5] Figures are presented for 1993-95 period. [6] Figures are presented for 1989-91 period and are not available for earlier. [7] Figures are presented for the 1985-87 period. [8] Figures are not available for the 1984-87 period. Note that Northern Ireland is considered separately from the rest of the UK (Great Britain) because different incentive schemes operate in each area.

Spatial Coverage

There is considerable variation in Western Europe with respect to spatial coverage, but little evidence that it has altered in response to greater foreign investment competition between countries. Examining 12 EU countries for the period 1988-96, spatial coverage increased in four, declined in three and did not change in another five Member States (Table

4.5). It should be noted that countries have limited scope for using spatial coverage to compete for foreign investment because of the need to gain European Commission approval on changes (as described in the next chapter), but despite this, the changes do not suggest rising competition.

Of the four countries that showed change, only two had dramatic rises: Germany and Italy, ironically two countries identified earlier as having relatively indifferent attitudes to the attraction of foreign investment. In Germany, the regional incentive map was expanded to cover the eastern *Länder* after unification because of their economic underdevelopment; but even after the increase in coverage, the share of German population in eligible areas was reduced again by the end of the period. By 1994, Italy had witnessed a significant increase in its spatial coverage, but this was linked to fundamental reform of Italian regional policy, which was refocused from an exclusive targeting of the *Mezzogiorno* region in the south to include industrial areas in the north suffering from industrial restructuring. Among the other countries, it is perhaps surprising to find spatial coverage declining in two of the countries most noted for their success in attracting foreign investment: the UK and the Netherlands.

Table 4.5 Spatial coverage, 1988-96 (share of population)

Country	1988	1990	1992	1994	1996
Belgium	33.1	33.1	33.1	33.1	35.0
France	39.0	41.9	41.9	41.9	40.9
Germany	32.8	34.8	42.5	38.2	38.2
Greece	100.0	100.0	100.0	100.0	100.0
Ireland	100.0	100.0	100.0	100.0	100.0
Italy	35.6	35.6	35.6	48.8	48.8
Luxembourg	100.0	100.0	79.7	79.7	42.7
Netherlands	25.0	19.9	19.9	16.6	15.6
Portugal	100.0	100.0	100.0	100.0	100.0
Spain	58.6	58.6	58.6	58.6	58.6
Sweden	13.5	8.0	8.0	13.5	13.5
UK	37.8	37.8	37.8	36.8	36.8

Source: Yuill, Bachtler and Wishlade, 1996.

Expenditure Levels

Expenditure on incentive schemes for attracting FDI varies greatly. The largest expenditure is in Italy and the eastern *Länder* of Germany - unusually, as both are not known for active FDI promotion policies - and the lowest in Luxembourg and Denmark (not surprising, given the size of their countries) (Wishlade *et al*, 1996). When calculated in terms of shares of GDP though, the highest concentrations of expenditure are in Luxembourg, Ireland, Greece, Portugal and the eastern *Länder* of Germany; France and Denmark have the lowest. The other wealthier countries of the EU tend to come in the middle of the ranking. In general, expenditure concentration seems inversely related to national GDP levels.

Nevertheless, it appears that the overall trends in spending on the main financial incentive schemes in recent years have been downward, largely in response to the need to reduce overall government expenditure (Table 4.6). Although cost-per-job data is confidential in national incentive schemes, it is possible to assess competition using per-capita expenditure figures. From these, it is clear that a steady decline has been taking place in the northern Community countries since 1980, especially in Denmark, the Netherlands and the UK, and to a lesser extent, in France, Ireland and the western *Länder* of Germany (though aid to the eastern *Länder* represents a notable exception). The southern European countries experienced rising expenditure during the 1980s, but more recently there have been signs that spending has been increasingly subjected to financial constraints.

Taking the different factors together, there is no clear relationship between expenditure and competition. While the less-developed countries of the EU (such as Greece, Ireland, Portugal and Spain) have wide scope for intense usage in terms of their maximum award ceilings and population coverage, they do not necessarily have the highest average award rates, as they generally do not have the resources to make full use of their incentive policy. Overall, the countries with the widest scope for using incentives to attract foreign investment are Greece and Ireland, those with the least may be the Netherlands and France. However, when comparing their scope for activity with their levels of investment, a link between the ability to use incentives and FDI flows cannot be established, as only Ireland in the first category has had notable success in attracting foreign investment, while

France and the Netherlands - with limited regional incentive capabilities -
are among the main destinations for foreign investment in Western Europe.

**Table 4.6 Expenditure on main financial incentives for selected
countries, 1980-93**

	Expenditure committed per capita in recipient regions (US$, 1993 prices, PPP)				
	1980	*1983*	*1986*	*1989*	*1993*
Belgium	48.3	61.4	58.7	76.4	34.1
France	19.8	16.2	10.7	8.2	n.a
Germany	35.5	43.1	40.6	67.8	n.a.
Ireland	130.5	54.8	77.5	94.5	n.a.
Italy	223.2	308.7	245.5	341.9	n.a.
Luxembourg	74.9	27.0	118.1	75.9	104.5
Netherlands	66.3	41.3	37.1	23.6	9.0
Portugal				35.8	65.5
Spain			12.0	41.0	n.a.
Sweden	89.3	100.7	114.9	122.8	79.2
Great Britain	75.6	93.2	75.7	44.2	27.9
N. Ireland	197.8	129.0	131.8	86.0	47.5

Source: Yuill, Bachtler and Wishlade, 1996.

As noted before, the best evidence for policy competition remains
principally anecdotal, though given the confidential nature of award offers,
such evidence has been difficult to assess because of the problems in
finding reliable information. Most relevant agencies will generally insist
that competition has not led to bidding wars. Where an agency does claim
that a rival successfully 'won' a project largely because of the incentive
package, the accusation is weakened by the agency's clear interest in
diminishing the strength of other locational determinants (such as the
quality of the workforce). Nevertheless, press reports of incentive offers to
companies continue to demonstrate how far governments are prepared to
bid for key projects. For example, it has been estimated that Hyundai's
US$ 5.7 billion semiconductor investment in Scotland in 1996 involved an
estimated cost-per-job as high as US$ 190,000 (the true figure has not been
released by the UK Government), though there is likely to be wide
variation within as well as between countries (*The Herald*, 1997).

Similarly, the 1991 offer of a US$ 680 million grant for the US$ 3.1 billion Ford/Volkswagen investment in Setúbal in Portugal was equivalent to about 7.3 percent of all European Structural Funds expenditure on economic development in Portugal between 1989 and 1992 (though it was paid out over a longer term) (*Corporate Location*, 1996c).

In general, few companies are prepared to discuss publicly the negotiations that take place with different agencies and the extent to which the agencies are 'played' off against each other. Evaluation is also complicated by the fact that companies are often prepared to point out that they did not select the location with the highest offer, but are less willing to indicate whether they would have chosen a particular location in the absence of the incentive package (even if it was smaller than rivals). Much can depend on the point at which incentives are brought to bear. For example, in the case of Hyundai's investment in Scotland, Germany and Austria were not included in the site shortlisting because of high production costs, although both offered the highest incentives - yet in the final selection between three locations in the UK and one in Ireland, it has been claimed that the UK's large incentive package offer *was* decisive in Ireland being ruled out (*Corporate Location*, 1996d).

Conclusions

The use of financial incentives is one of the principal policy areas where it is clear that there is policy competition in Western Europe. Apart from Denmark, all the major Western European countries offer financial incentives to large investment projects - and in practice, these seem to be mainly interpreted as mobile FDI projects, though few incentive schemes make explicit reference. Indeed, regional financial incentives are widely regarded as the key policy instrument for attracting foreign investment in Western Europe.

Having established the existence of competition though, the impact of such rivalry remains difficult to assess. Two types of uncertainty make it nearly impossible to evaluate satisfactorily the effects of policy competition. First, it is not clear how effective incentives are in influencing location decisions. While research consistently places incentives low on the list of determining factors, major investments in

Western Europe - as in other parts of the world - are still accompanied by significant incentive awards, especially for greenfield locations. On a case-by-case basis, it may be possible in some circumstances to ascertain whether the incentives influenced the choice of region within countries (as between assisted against non-assisted areas) as well as between countries. Nevertheless, generalising for investment decisions as a whole has been fraught with what appear to be fundamental methodological problems. By their very nature, regional incentive offers are so specific and individual in their design and application that it may not be possible to make such generalisations, raising questions as to the rationale for pursuing policies that cannot be subject to proper evaluation.

The second uncertainty regards the availability and reliability of data. Grant decisions (and often, values) are subject to commercial confidentiality. Accusations of bidding wars between agencies are difficult to substantiate because of the vested interests of agencies in concealing the role of their own grant offers and exaggerating the role of their rivals' (thereby diminishing the importance of other, more influential location factors).

Similarly, the question of whether policy competition has worsened cannot be adequately answered. There are clearly more organisations involved in FDI promotion than ever before across Europe, as demonstrated by the rise in the number of national and regional agencies and their networks of offices. However, greater organisational competition has not translated into a competitive spiral of policy changes, as measured by alterations to award ceilings, spatial coverage limits and regional incentive expenditure over the past decade. This is in large part a tribute to the controls on regional incentive spending that operate at Community level, which are discussed in the following chapter.

In spite of the limited effects of policy competition, the scope for outbidding and the uncertainty regarding the efficacy of regional incentives has led to wider debate on the future use of incentives in FDI promotion. Policy recommendations in numerous research studies have suggested non-incentive approaches should be employed in attracting and keeping foreign investment. For example, it has been argued that incentives should be refined and targeted in order to increase the spillover and dynamic effects of foreign investment by encouraging the location of higher value-added corporate activities (Amin and Tomaney, 1995), or that the payment of incentives should be tied to more rigorous measures of plant performance in terms of job and local content purchasing (Shirlow, 1995). These are discussed in more detail in the concluding chapter of this report.

Such has been the competition for foreign investment in the EU and the importance of short-term job creation in many national and regional development strategies, it has been difficult for governments to scale down the use of incentives. Although most agencies and investors play down the influence of incentives in investment decisions, few appear ready to abandon their use. Rather, in the likely continuing absence of cost-benefit analyses of regional incentives, there remains a risk that increasing competition for foreign investment projects - not least from CEE countries - could drive up incentive spending.

As noted before, the best evidence for policy competition remains principally anecdotal, though given the confidential nature of award offers, such evidence has been difficult to assess because of the problems in finding reliable information. Most relevant agencies will generally insist that competition has not led to bidding wars. Where an agency does claim that a rival successfully 'won' a project largely because of the incentive package, the accusation is weakened by the agency's clear interest in diminishing the strength of other locational determinants (such as the quality of the workforce). Nevertheless, press reports of incentive offers to companies continue to demonstrate how far governments are prepared to bid for key projects. For example, it has been estimated that Hyundai's US$ 5.7 billion semiconductor investment in Scotland in 1996 involved an estimated cost-per-job as high as US$ 190,000 (the true figure has not been released by the UK Government), though there is likely to be wide variation within as well as between countries (*The Herald*, 1997). Similarly, the 1991 offer of a US$ 680 million grant for the US$ 3.1 billion Ford/Volkswagen investment in Setúbal in Portugal was equivalent to about 7.3 percent of all European Structural Funds expenditure on economic development in Portugal between 1989 and 1992 (though it was paid out over a longer term) (*Corporate Location*, 1996c).

In general, few companies are prepared to discuss publicly the negotiations that take place with different agencies and the extent to which the agencies are 'played' off against each other. Evaluation is also complicated by the fact that companies are often prepared to point out that they did not select the location with the highest offer, but are less willing to indicate whether they would have chosen a particular location in the absence of the incentive package (even if it was smaller than rivals). Much can depend on the point at which incentives are brought to bear. For example, in the case of Hyundai's investment in Scotland, Germany and Austria were not included in the site shortlisting because of high production costs, although both offered the highest incentives - yet in the final selection between three locations in the UK and one in Ireland, it has been claimed that the UK's large incentive package offer *was* decisive in Ireland being ruled out (*Corporate Location*, 1996d).

5 Incentives Regulation

FIONA WISHLADE

Introduction

In recent years, the control of financial incentives in Europe has attracted considerable attention. In part, this can be attributed to a small number of high profile cases such as those involving particularly sensitive sectors (notably steel) or large individual firms, such as British Aerospace and Rover, Crédit Lyonnais and the major flag-carrier airlines. More fundamentally, however, the so-called '1992 deadline' for the completion of the Single European Market moved the issue of subsidies – State aids in EU-speak - higher up the policy agenda. A number of influential reports (Cecchini, 1988; Padoa-Schioppa *et al*, 1987) had stressed the importance of tighter control on subsidies in the context of an 'internal market'; the absence of other forms of protectionism (like preferential public procurement or discriminatory product standards) outlawed under the Single Market programme was considered to have the potential to magnify the distorting effects of those subsidies that were offered and to increase the temptation for European governments to react to increased competition by introducing more aid to protect or promote national industries.

Whilst it is certainly true that there has been a resurgence of interest and activity in the control of subsidies since the late 1980s, it is important to remember that the basis for Community policy in this area is the 1957 Treaty founding the European Economic Community[1]. The inclusion of provisions on the control of State aids reflects an early recognition on the part of the authors of the Treaty that uncontrolled subsidies could

---

[1] The European Economic Community came into being with the signature of the Treaty of Rome in 1957. This Treaty was substantially revised in 1985 by the Single European Act and in 1992 by the Maastricht Treaty (the Treaty on European Union). Neither of these revisions significantly altered the substance of the State aids rules.

undermine the achievement of a common market. More than 35 years on, the original provisions remain substantially unchanged.

The provisions of the Treaty with regard to State aids are neutral with respect to nationality and ownership. In other words, foreign direct investment is not targeted by the rules on State aids and the rules apply to private and nationalised enterprises. Nevertheless, as will be seen, the perceived risks of competitive outbidding for internationally-mobile investment has been an important motivating force behind the development of substantive rules on State aid control. Against this background, this chapter first considers the general context for the control of incentives in Europe; the second part focuses on the control of regional financial incentives, which, as explained in Chapter 4, have become the main incentives used to attract FDI; the third part reviews some of the options for controlling incentives for FDI; the concluding section considers some of the challenges facing future policy development.

The Basic Principles of State Aid Control in the EU

The key parts of the Treaty with respect to State aids are Articles 92 and 93. Article 92 provides for a general ban on so-called 'State aids', but goes on to outline certain exceptions to this ban; Article 93 defines the role of the European Commission in controlling State aids, providing it with wide-ranging discretionary powers to decide what the exceptions to the general prohibition should be. An interesting feature of Article 92 is that, although it bans State aids, it does not define, in any prescriptive sense, what State aids actually are (this was almost certainly intentional given the powers accorded to the Commission under Article 93); nevertheless, it is clear that the scope of Article 92 is extremely wide.

Definition of 'State Aid'

First, the aid can be 'in any form whatsoever'. This has been shown to include not only obvious incentive types like grants and soft loans, but also the provision of site-specific infrastructure to firms, the writing-off of the losses of public undertakings, subscriptions to share capital or the sale of land at below cost. For the Commission, the key test of whether a transaction amounts to aid is the 'commercial investor principle' - in other words, would the firm have been able to obtain the sums concerned from a commercial source?

The second feature of an aid is that it is 'granted by a Member State or through State resources'. Again, a wide interpretation has been given to the Treaty and it is now clear that Article 92 concerns the activities of all public bodies, or private agencies acting on their behalf, at national, regional and local levels.

The third characteristic of an aid under Article 92 is that it must 'distort or threaten to distort competition'. This might appear to limit the scope of Article 92; in practice, however, the increasing interdependence of European markets has made it relatively easy to assert that there is a threat to actual or potential competition.

Last, to fall within the scope of Article 92, State aids must distort or threaten to distort competition 'by favouring certain undertakings or the production of certain goods'. This requirement draws a distinction between measures of general economic policy, on the one hand, and measures which directly or indirectly assist certain firms or industries, on the other.

Powers of the European Commission

The Commission's powers in the control of State aids are exercised through its competition policy directorate, DGIV; the Commission arguably has more discretion and autonomy in this sphere than in any other area of Community policy. Of key importance, Member States must notify the Commission, in advance, of any plans to offer aid[2]. Moreover, it is for the Commission, and *not* the Member States to decide whether a measure constitutes an aid, and, if so, whether it qualifies for one of the exemptions from the general ban. The vast majority of aid awards are made under aid schemes, rather than involving *ad hoc* support for individual firms. However, both aid schemes and individual awards made outside of aid schemes must be notified. Commission approval of an aid scheme is effectively a 'block exemption' from notification for individual awards under that programme, provided that these are made according to the conditions notified and approved.

---

[2]The only exception to this is the *de minimis* rule which provides that aid of less than ECU 100,000 over three years need not be notified.

The Commission's approach is, however, far from passive. It monitors the media for reports of aid paid and can require Member States to provide details of individual cases. The Commission also follows up complaints from aggrieved competitors who believe that aid has been paid out unlawfully. The penalties for not notifying can be high; unnotified aid is deemed to be illegal and the recipient firm may be required to repay the sums received, plus interest, even if this puts the firm's viability at risk. Moreover, the Commission has had consistent backing from the European Court of Justice in requiring repayment. In addition to its role with respect to new aid notifications and the following-up of complaints, the Commission can also review aid schemes approved in the past and require amendments to them.

Commission decisions can be challenged in the European courts, but in practice the scope to do so is limited. The main reason for this is the Commission's quasi-judicial role in assessing the compatibility of aids with the Treaty; in consequence, the main grounds for legal action against the Commission in this field have been procedural irregularity. Not surprisingly, the Commission has been increasingly careful to ensure that procedural requirements are complied with.

A final point to note about the role of the Commission in the field of subsidies is that it is one of the few areas in which it can act independently of the Council of Ministers. As might be expected, the extensive powers and independence of the Commission in this arena, combining, as it does, the roles of legislator, policeman, prosecutor and judge, has led to considerable antagonism between DGIV and the Member States.

Commission Policy in Different State Aid Areas

The core of Commission policy on State aids is its interpretation of Article 92(3) of the Treaty. This gives the Commission the power to decide which aids can be exempted from the general prohibition imposed by Article 92(1). This discretion is used to try to balance the possible distortion of competition arising from the aid against the beneficial effects that the aid could have. This has involved extensive development of the basic Treaty provisions by the Commission; increasingly, this has taken the form of published guidelines and frameworks for different aid areas[3]. For the most part, these serve to clarify the ways in which the Commission will exercise its discretion and to encourage Member States to notify the information required[4].

Commission guidelines and frameworks divide into three broad groups:

- *sectoral* rules, that is, those concerned with assistance to industries that are deemed to be in 'overcapacity' in the EU (this includes the motor industry and synthetic fibres);
- *horizontal* rules, that is, those concerned with particular types of expenditure, such as research and development, and environmental protection; and
- rules covering assistance for *general investment*, that is, items such as land, buildings, plant and equipment.

Under the *sectoral* frameworks (the details of which differ from industry to industry) the common theme is that aid for investment which would increase the output of the goods concerned should be strictly limited or even prohibited completely. The motor industry framework, for example, requires that all cases of aid to projects involving investments of more than ECU 17 million be notified to the Commission individually. The Commission then weighs the possible harm to the sector of providing a subsidy against the possible benefits to be gained (for example, from inducing the plant to locate in an area of high unemployment, rather than a central, prosperous location) before deciding whether to authorise aid and at what level.

As noted above, *horizontal* frameworks are concerned with particular types of expenditure for a particular end. The research and development aid framework, for example, defines the different stages of the R&D process and the maximum levels of award which the Commission will

---

[3] These are generally published in the Official Journal of the European Communities as they appear and are collected in CEC (1995c) *Competition Law in the European Communities, Volume IIA: Rules Applicable to State Aids,* Office for Official Publications of the European Communities, Luxembourg.

[4] However, some rules are mandatory, notably those relating to coal and steel, transport, agriculture and fisheries, and shipbuilding.

usually authorise for the different phases. As such, the framework is a clear expression of how the Commission will treat R&D aid programmes notified to it and gives Member States some guidelines as to how an aid programme should be designed if it is to be accepted by the Commission. There is some scope for discrimination against large firms insofar as R&D aid to very large projects must be notified individually, but in general, the Commission's approach to support for R&D is a positive one.

As far as *general investment aid* is concerned, two main sets of rules come into play: those concerning investment aid to small and medium-sized firms; and those concerning general investment aid under regional policy. The key point to note as far as *mobile* investments are concerned is that these rules virtually exclude the possibility of providing investment aid to large firms unless they are located in designated problem regions. Related, largely as a consequence of Community competition policy, regional incentive policy has become the key financial incentive instrument for attracting mobile investment in Europe.

Community Competition Rules and State Aids for Mobile Investments

There are no rules relating specifically to subsidies for mobile investments in the EU. On the other hand, since the 1960s, the issue of competition for mobile investment has been the driving force behind the development of Commission policy in controlling general investment aid, and, in particular, regional aid[5]. Moreover, it was as a result of concerns about competitive outbidding for mobile investment between regions that regional aid was the first policy area in which the Commission sought to formalise its approach to subsidy control. In turn, a consequence of Commission action has been the reinforcement of the position of regional aids as the key incentives for attracting mobile investments.

The Commission first proposed a system for coordinating regional aids in 1968; this culminated in the adoption in 1971 of the first set of

---

[5] '...one of the objectives of the co-ordination and adaptation of general systems of regional aid is to put an end to the outbidding between Member States in order to attract investments to their respective territories...' Council Resolution of 20 October 1971 on General Systems of Regional Aid; Official Journal of the European Communities, No. C111, 4.11.1971.

principles for coordinating regional assistance[6]. These first principles were supplemented in 1975 and 1979 (CEC, 1975 and 1979). Together the three documents addressed a number of key issues relating to the control of regional incentives, notably: the need to restrict regional aids to areas affected by economic problems; the need to set maximum award values and link these ceilings to the severity of economic problems in an area; the need to develop a common basis for assessing the value of incentives; and the need for transparency in the type of incentives offered. In 1988, these documents were further supplemented by the Commission's methodology for approving the regional aid maps of the Member States (CEC, 1988).

These four documents form the basis for the assessment of regional aid policies in the EU. There are two key features of the Commission approach to disciplining regional incentives: first, its control over the spatial coverage of regional policy; and second, its influence over incentive values.

Controlling Regional Aids: Spatial Coverage

At the core of Commission policy on controlling regional aids are issues of spatial coverage. When introducing new regional aid schemes, or changing existing ones, Member States must also submit a map of the areas in which policy is to be available; like other aspects of aid policy, the map must be approved before it is implemented. In addition, the Commission can at any time review regional aid maps that it has approved in the past, and propose a cutback in coverage.

Details of the Commission approach to approving regional aid maps were first made public in the 1988 communication 'in order to promote a greater understanding and transparency of the decisions taken by the Commission under Articles 92 and 93 with respect to national regional aid systems'. It is questionable whether much understanding has been achieved. Prior to 1988, Member State criticism centred on Commission secrecy about its methodology; disclosure of the methodology provided Member States with considerable ammunition to attack the substance of

---

[6] Council Resolution of 20 October 1971 on General Systems of Regional Aid; Official Journal of the European Communities, No. C111, 4.11.1971.

policy. The grounds for criticism are different; but the level of criticism is probably greater.

The Commission's methodology has been described in detail elsewhere (Yuill *et al*, 1997) and need only be outlined here. It distinguishes between areas exempted from the general ban on aids by virtue of Article 92(3)(a), the 'least-favoured regions', and those exempted on the basis of Article 92(3)(c), hereafter referred to as 'development areas'.

Designation of Least-Favoured Regions

Designation as a least-favoured region is based on the so-called NUTS Level II[7] region as a geographical unit. The analysis uses *per capita* GDP data, adjusted to allow for differences in the cost of living between Member States. Least-favoured regions are deemed to be those where GDP per head is less than or equal to 75 percent of the EU average. The result of applying this methodology is that all of Greece, Ireland and Portugal, most of Spain and the south of Italy are designated as least-favoured regions.

Designation of Development Areas

A key difference between least-favoured regions and development areas is that the former are designated solely with reference to average GDP per head in the EU. In contrast, the designation of development areas involves assessing the prosperity of a region within a country *and* the prosperity of the country within the EU. This is done by setting national levels of GDP per head and unemployment are against the EU average to produce a threshold or index for each indicator, for each country[8]. The result is that, within richer countries, the coverage of assisted areas authorised on the basis of the methodology will be less than in poorer countries.

---

[7] *Nomenclature des unites territoriales statistiques*, geographical units used for EU statistical purposes. NUTS I is the national level; NUTS II is equivalent to an Italian region or the Autonomous Community in Spain.
[8] These indices are updated periodically and published in the Official Journal of the European Communities.

In designating the development areas, smaller geographical units are used, the so-called NUTS Level III[9] region. To qualify, an area must have GDP per head at least 15 percent below the national index and/or an unemployment rate of at least 10 percent above the national index.

A further key difference between this and the designation methodology for the least-favoured regions is that this first quantitative stage is inconclusive. In a second, more discretionary phase of scrutiny (which can include regions that do and regions that do not qualify on the basis of the quantitative assessment), the Commission can take account of a range of other factors, such as the trend and structure of unemployment, net migration, demographic pressure, geographical situation, topography, infrastructure, etc.

The 1995 enlargement to include Finland and Sweden resulted in a new criterion for development area status. An alternative to the GDP and unemployment test is a population density test. NUTS III regions with fewer than 12.5 inhabitants per km^2 may also qualify as development areas.

As a consequence of Commission intervention, most of the northern Member States have been forced to cut back on the coverage of areas eligible for regional aid. It is not surprising, then, that the methodology described above is the source of much controversy and has been at the heart of a number of long-standing disputes between the Commission and national governments.

Although much of the criticism is apparently of a technical nature, focusing on issues related to the size of geographical units and the type of indicators used, underlying this is a fundamental antipathy towards Commission intervention in national policy-making. There is considerable resentment that DGIV's use of both quantitative and qualitative criteria affords the Commission considerable room for manoeuvre; some national policy-makers view the quantitative stage merely as providing the Commission with an apparently objective justification for decisions which are essentially subjective. This perception is heightened by the nature of the approval process for assisted area maps (Yuill *et al*, 1994).

In this context, it is important to note that informal contact is often key in discussions over new assisted area maps. Some Member States 'sound

---

[9]NUTS III is equivalent to the *departement* in France or an English county.

out' DGIV in advance to identify potential areas of disagreement over proposed new maps in order to ensure that, following formal notification, approval is swift and smooth. Others have forced the hand of DGIV by formally notifying and making public their proposed assisted area maps at the same time, thereby shifting the responsibility for the eventual outcome to the Commission (this is a useful tactic if cutbacks are likely to prove domestically unpopular). Similarly, others have notified maps in full knowledge that the coverage proposed is too extensive to be acceptable but have redirected the potential criticism of local politicians by making the Commission the final arbiter. Also, apparently unrelated issues have a role to play; it is not uncommon for the announcement of the Commission Decision on regional aid maps to be held over until after elections in a Member State. Moreover, controversial Commission decisions were notable by their absence during the ratification process of the Maastricht Treaty. In all, the whole process is highly politicised. Indeed, disputes over assisted area maps are often resolved at the highest political level between national ministers and the Commissioner for Competition Policy. All this contrasts sharply with the apparently objective process of designating areas on the basis of income and unemployment.

More recently, there are signs that the controversy over the system for approving areas is abating. Over the last four years or so, the emphasis in DGIV's approach to assessing areas has shifted away from an analysis of the situation in individual regions and has focused more on the proportion of the national population in designated assisted areas. The starting point for this approach has been the setting of a population ceiling for assisted areas for each country; within this ceiling, Member States have more freedom to choose assisted areas, although the 1988 methodology described above still has some bearing on what the Commission will approve. In consequence, recent reviews of assisted areas have been concluded with much less acrimony than in the past. However, this may be because the Commission has been less successful in imposing its views of late; both the French and the German governments (notorious for their long-running disputes with DGIV) were able to negotiate significant increases in the population ceilings DGIV had set before going on to designate assisted areas on their own terms.

Controlling Regional Aids: Award Values

The second strand in the Commission approach to controlling regional aids (and, therefore, support for mobile investment) is to stipulate the maximum levels of assistance that can be offered. In broad terms, the distinction between the least-favoured regions and the development areas is retained for the purposes of setting rates of award.

In the least-favoured regions, investment aid of up to 75 percent net grant-equivalent[10] of eligible expenditure[11] may be authorised by the Commission. In the development areas, the maximum authorised does not generally exceed 30 percent net grant-equivalent. In practice, however, the actual maxima authorised by the Commission vary widely within these ceilings.

In general terms, this aspect of Commission intervention is much less controversial than its control of the geographical coverage of regional policy. The main reason for this is that the Commission ceilings tend not to constrain programme administrators making grant offers to firms. On the contrary, as shown in Table 4.3 in the previous chapter, average awards under the main regional incentive programmes are very considerably below the maxima authorised. Of course, average figures should be viewed with caution. Moreover, regional aid schemes are not solely directed at multinationals, but mobile projects are generally likely to receive higher rates of award than domestic projects, because of their intrinsic bargaining power. Nevertheless, from interviews with national policy-makers, it is clear that, in *some* countries, the maximum rate is never offered, no matter how attractive the project.

In consequence, the ceilings authorised by the Commission are largely theoretical and of limited impact in terms of disciplining regional aids. Of considerably more importance in influencing award values have been the

---

[10] This refers to the value of the incentive after tax; however, there is considerable variation in the tax treatment of regional incentives. For details see Yuill, Bachtler and Wishlade (1997).

[11] The Commission's eligible expenditure ceilings are calculated with reference to spending on fixed assets - land, buildings, plant and equipment. This does not mean that countries cannot assist other types of expenditure but rather that maximum aid levels are related to capital spending. It is worth noting that many countries do not subsidise the purchase of land under regional aid programmes.

growing budgetary constraints under which regional policy-makers have had to operate. As a result, programme administrators have become increasingly selective about which projects to assist, and there has been growing emphasis on obtaining 'value for money' from regional aids by not awarding more than is thought necessary to attract a given project.

It is surprising that the Commission should have paid relatively little attention to modulating maximum award values, especially given the relatively well-developed (albeit contested) approach to approving assisted areas. Moreover, there is no rational basis for the maximum award levels authorised; the starting point for the Commission principles devised in the early 1970s were the rates already being offered by the Member States. Subsequent decisions over the past two decades have simply built on this precedent, but without any systematic attempt to relate maximum award values to the severity of the regional problem.

It could be argued that, since the Commission ceilings do not bite, the absence of a rationale for its authorisation of maximum award values is unimportant. However, the different ceilings are intended to reflect the severity of the regional problem and 'level the playing field' by maintaining the competitive advantage of the least-favoured areas in the attraction of mobile projects; the fact that the ceilings do not bite erodes that advantage. Related, the countries that are authorised to offer high rates (up to 75 percent of capital investment) in their problem regions are, in general, precisely the ones that lack the budgetary resources to do so. (The rationale for a 75 percent ceiling is anyway highly questionable and is widely viewed as excessive.) Even at rates of award well below the authorised ceilings, the *volume* of subsidy paid to a single project can be significant. For example, the subsidy offered to the Ford/Volkswagen joint-venture in Portugal in 1991 totalled some US\$ 610 million (ECU 500 million), but this represented only 32.8 percent (gross) of eligible investment in an area where the Commission ceiling was 75 percent (net).

Controlling Subsidies for Mobile Investment: Issues and Options

The discussion above has focused on Commission control of regional aids (the main source of investment aid for mobile projects) noting that concern at competitive outbidding led the Commission to target regional aids early on. It is, however, questionable to what extent the Commission has influenced the 'blind auction' process that characterises negotiations between mobile investors and potential host countries. Certainly, competition for inward investment among European countries remains fierce and most governments are secretive about the levels of aid used to attract such projects. An important factor in determining levels of grant offered to mobile projects is the value of offers thought to have been made elsewhere; the growing emphasis on obtaining value for money from regional policy is a far more limiting factor than the Commission's award ceilings. In short, Commission control of regional aids has been distinctly 'one-dimensional', focusing on restricting *where* incentives can be offered, but having little influence on *how much* they are worth.

The relative absence of control over award values has caused concern in a number of quarters. Three options for exercising control over award values have come in for consideration: controlling *expenditure* on regional aids; controlling awards to highly *capital-intensive* projects; and controlling *large* individual awards.

Regional Aid Spending

Regarding regional aid *expenditure*, the main issue has been the inability of the less prosperous countries to finance aid at the levels authorised, with the result that their 'competitive edge' in terms of higher award values for attracting mobile projects is eroded. The scale of the disparities in spending can be derived from the Commission's regular reports on State aid spending in recipient regions in the Community (CEC, 1997b; Yuill *et al*, 1994). Greece, Portugal, Ireland and Spain all have *per capita* GDP well under the Community average and all spend significantly less than the average on regional aid. In contrast, German levels of GDP per head are well above the average but *per capita* regional aid spending is around ten times that for Portugal.

However, policy-makers from the less prosperous countries are not alone in criticising the Commission for not taking account of spending levels. One French regional policy-maker has commented that 'when DGIV re-examines subsidy systems in richer countries, it tends to operate only in terms of population covered and completely ignores...the level of budgetary resources dedicated to such systems...' (Chicoye, 1992). This is perhaps not a surprising criticism in the French context since France is consistently at or near the bottom of the ranking of regional aid spending per head of national population, but has very extensive assisted area coverage which the French authorities are under constant Commission pressure to reduce.

Although the budget assigned to a particular scheme must be notified at the same time as the scheme itself, the Commission has not sought to control budgets and the level of spending rarely seems to be an issue between Member States and the Commission[12]. In any case, such control would be highly unpopular with the Member States and strikes at the heart of national sovereignty and issues of policy choice. In addition, there would be major practical and methodological considerations in deciding what an appropriate regional policy budget for a given country would be. Further, there is some doubt whether the Commission even has the jurisdiction to impose regional policy budget limits on countries[13].

On the other hand, action to control budgets could barely be more unpopular than the control exerted over the assisted areas, which already limits national policy options. There is considerable experience in calculating appropriate budgets for the purposes of the Community's own regional development policy (albeit through a highly politicised process). Last, with regard to issues of jurisdiction, the Treaty makes no mention of the Commission prescribing assisted area coverage or levels of award, but rather casts the control of incentives in the context of a general prohibition to which exceptions may be made. It is difficult to see why this could not be used to limit regional aid budgets on the basis that expenditure below a certain level would not 'affect trading conditions to an extent contrary to the common interest'.

---

[12] One recent exception to this concerns the extension of funding for Italian regional incentive policy; the Commission set a limit on spending under the then current programme and stipulated that any further spending had to be under a modified aid programme (Official Journal of the European Communities, No. L 117, 13.5.93).

[13] Interview with Commission official, DGIV, by the author.

Awards to Capital-Intensive Investments

The second area of concern with respect to award values is in respect of aids to highly capital-intensive projects. Following the acceptance of a Communication (CEC, 1990) on industrial policy issues the Commission began work on devising rules to regulate such incentives. Commission concern centres on two factors. First, it considers that the higher the capital investment in relation to job creation, to increased production capacity, or to value-added, then the greater the distortion of competition. Second, it takes the view that incentives to highly capital-intensive projects do not contribute significantly to the policies under which they are offered. Associated with this, it argues that assistance to capital-intensive projects results in a lower level of job creation overall than could be obtained with a more balanced distribution of government incentives.

According to the Communication, 'it is not so much the *quantity* of aid granted as the importance of the *differential* between existing aid schemes which acts as the spur for footloose industrial location' (emphases added). It further proposes that the poorer countries could make substantial budgetary savings if the appropriate differentials were maintained at a lower level.

Reflecting these issues, consideration was given to finding a method which would reduce the *value* of incentives without affecting maximum *rates* of award. The proposals involved setting cost-per-job limits to investment eligible for incentives. This proved highly controversial and left Member States and different Directorates of the Commission deeply divided.

Certainly, there were a number of obvious problems with the approach. In particular, the Commission's view that it is the rate differential and not the quantity of aid which is central to locational choice is questionable. In addition, such an approach would tend to discriminate between sectors; this could restrict aid where little or no distortion was involved in one sector, whilst leaving a less capital-intensive sector unaffected. Also, highly-capital intensive projects are sought after precisely because capital-intensity is often associated with high-value new technologies that can bring benefits to the problem regions; cost-per-job limits could reduce the value of the aid on offer to such projects in the problem regions, making such areas attractive only for labour-intensive, lower technology activities. Further, a straight calculation based on jobs associated in the investing firm takes no account of indirect job creation or local linkages. There are also practical problems; incentive applicants consistently overestimate the number of jobs likely to be created. This approach would encourage that tendency, raising complicated issues for subsequent monitoring and possible repayment of incentive awards. Last, taking a wider view, there is the issue of whether such limits would make a European location less attractive in a global context.

For these reasons, the proposed capital intensity framework met with a mixed reaction. At the national levels, for example, Spain and Germany were opposed to such regulation[14]. In contrast, the UK government regarded 'effective constraints on "subsidy auctions" for internationally mobile investment projects' as a priority and 'was pressing the Commission to adopt its proposal to limit aid for capital intensive projects' (HMSO, 1994).

Reflecting the lack of agreement, the capital intensity proposals were superseded by the consideration of other options, in particular, proposals to consider individually any awards over a given size.

Large Individual Awards

A further issue with respect to award values concerns large individual awards. As noted earlier, aids can attain very high volumes whilst remaining well within the authorised ceilings. This has led some to argue that a more restrictive approach is needed. The Confederation of British Industry, for example, has suggested that 'the Commission should introduce a formal notification system for any large awards of aid under a scheme which has already been approved' (CBI, 1994); the CBI also considers that the percentage ceilings for regional aid are anyway set too high.

Information on individual awards under approved schemes is difficult to obtain and tends to emerge anecdotally from press reports or parliamentary questions rather than being available systematically[15]. For

---

[14] Interviews with national policy-makers by the author.
[15] New rules introduced by the Commission in 1994 will require information on larger awards under approved programmes to be submitted in the annual report on

this reason, it is difficult to take a view on what might be considered a 'large award', or whether the 'trigger' should be the size of the investment, and whether the notion of a large award should vary by sector.

There are precedents for individual notifications under approved programmes in the context of sectors considered to be in 'overcapacity'. For example, the synthetic fibres code requires prior notification and Commission approval of all awards to producers of goods defined in the code; and the motor industry framework requires this for all plans to aid investments exceeding ECU 17 million (CEC, 1992a and 1989).

These requirements to notify create an opportunity for the Commission to assess the possible benefits of assistance against the risk of distorting trade or increasing overcapacity. However, such individual decisions are often highly controversial. The Commission decision not to oppose French government aid to Allied Signal was challenged before the European Court of Justice and the decision overturned[16]; as a result, the Commission sought repayment of some ECU 30 million. Similarly, the decision to allow aid to the Ford/Volkswagen joint-venture in Portugal was challenged by a French competitor, Matra. In this instance, however, the Court found for the Commission[17]. More recently, European textile and clothing manufacturers lodged a complaint against the Commission for allowing UK grant aid of £61 million to a £157 million investment by the Taiwanese textile firm Hualon. These cases are just a small sample of FDI aid cases that have made headline news in the financial press. Looking beyond regional aid decisions, recent cases involving aids to various European airlines, the steel industry and support for the restructuring of Bull and Bremer Vulkan and the media response to these are indicative of just how sensitive decisions relating to individual firms can be, especially if national interests are involved (*The Economist*, 1994).

The extent to which apparently extraneous issues and pressures from national governments have influenced these and other Commission decisions has led some to argue for an independent agency to oversee State

---

programme implementation. However, the contents of these reports are not made public and it seems unlikely that they would be in the future.

[16] *CIRFS v Commission* ('Allied Signal'), Case No. C 373/89, judgement of 24 March 1993.

[17] *Matra v Commission*, Case No. 225/91, judgement of 15 June 1993.

aids (*The Economist*, 1992). Given this context, the introduction of a system that would increase Commission involvement in individual award decisions, and potentially make it the arbiter in incentives for major mobile investments would require considerable thought.

Conclusions

The first part of this chapter outlined an apparently formidable array of powers for controlling subsidies in the EU. So-called State aids are outlawed by the founding Treaty of the EEC, subject to certain exceptions; the definition of those exceptions is the exclusive preserve of the European Commission. All aids must be notified to the Commission in advance and approved before implementation; unnotified aid is illegal and may have to be repaid (with interest), regardless of national laws on legitimate expectation and irrespective of whether it puts the firm in jeopardy. The Commission can propose changes to aid schemes and can render a scheme illegal if the Member State refuses to co-operate. It monitors the press for reports of subsidies paid and investigates claims from governments and aggrieved competitors; in so doing, it can require governments to provide information. Its decisions can be challenged in the Court of First Instance (by firms) or in the European Court of Justice (by Member States), but successful challenges on the substance of decisions are rare.

The second part discussed subsidy control policy with respect to mobile projects. Although such projects are not explicitly targeted by Commission policy, the risks of competitive outbidding for mobile investments have been the main motivation behind the control of general investment aid. This is reflected in two factors: first, that regional aid policies were the first to be disciplined within a framework of rules; and second, that the Commission has, in parallel, progressively tightened the circumstances in which general investment can be subsidised. This means that the Community's rules virtually exclude the possibility of providing general investment subsidies to large firms, unless they are located in designated regional development areas approved as such by the Commission. In consequence, the regional incentive policies of the Member States have been subject to close scrutiny and regulation over the past 25 years or so. In this context, the Commission has not only constrained the spatial coverage of regional policy, but also set ceilings on the incentives that countries can offer.

On paper, then, the Community approach to disciplining subsidies contains the key elements needed to ensure effective control of incentives. Moreover, the Commission claims success in having reduced levels of spending on subsidies in the EU[18]. There are, however, a number of significant weaknesses that actually or potentially undermine this system of control.

Of particular relevance to mobile projects, the discussion above suggested that control of award values under regional aid programmes has little rational basis and is relatively ineffective in terms of curbing the volume of subsidy. As a result, high levels of assistance can be offered quite legitimately in many locations. In consequence, there would appear to be a strong case for revisiting the aid ceilings currently in force, as well as giving serious consideration to other options for controlling award values.

A further issue of relevance to support for mobile projects concerns economic development policy trends within EU countries. The past decade has seen the growing involvement of regional and local governments and development agencies in the attraction of inward investment. Many of these provide financial assistance in the form of tax breaks, cheap land, site infrastructure (all of which count as 'State aid') as well as direct grant-based support. This is often negotiated on an *ad hoc* basis and it is often not clear whether such incentives have been notified and approved by the Commission. Moreover, there is some evidence that local policy-makers and politicians are unaware of the rules governing subsidies; press reports of local successes in attracting foreign investments are frequently the starting point for Commission investigations of illegal subsidies.

Related to this is a more general weakness; it is to the *national* authorities that Commission inquiries, and ultimately Decisions, are addressed, rather than the authority allegedly offering the subsidy. Thus, the investigation of the sale of land by Derbyshire County Council to

---

[18] The Commission refers to the 'globally good results which have been achieved through its State Aid control in recent years' (CEC, 1992b). However, it is highly questionable to what extent falling expenditure is attributable to *Commission* action rather than *national* policy decisions.

Toyota culminated in a Decision addressed to the UK government requiring reimbursement of the subsidy involved in the sale. In this case the Commission was successful, but national governments have little or no motivation to pursue local bodies for details of aid paid. Often they simply transmit the response to the Commission, while attaching little credence to it themselves[19]. More generally, there is some concern about the lack of rigour with which complaints from competitors and Member States are sometimes pursued. The initial stage of the investigation is usually a request for information from the national government concerned. However, some policy-makers have commented that they have been able to satisfy these inquiries with relatively little information together with general assurances of compliance; on the other hand, complainants have remarked on their dissatisfaction with the level of detail fed back to them by the Commission[20].

The perfunctory way in which *some* inquiries appear to be pursued is probably partly due to lack of resources. The tale that there are more staff involved in giving aid in Wallonia (a region of Belgium) than there are controlling aids across the Community may be apocryphal, but DGIV is notoriously short of resources for its role in disciplining State aids (Wilks, 1992).

There is then some scope for evading Commission scrutiny, although one can only speculate at the scale of evasion that actually takes place. On the other hand, it could be argued that there is still relatively little motivation for Member States to notify aid proposals (particularly individual awards), especially if there is some doubt about whether the Commission would ultimately approve the subsidy. Indeed, the more objectionable the subsidy (from the Commission's perspective) the greater the temptation simply to risk subsequent discovery. If the aid were later to be found unlawful (and the Commission must establish this on the substance of the case), then repayment could be required; however, even if it were, the objective of the subsidy might already have been attained (for example, attracting the mobile project or keeping a firm in business). Moreover, recent reports show the recovery record to be relatively poor; in

---

[19] Interviews with national policy-makers by the author.
[20] Interviews with national policy-makers by the author.

only 13 cases (out of 46 orders) was repayment secured between 1982 and 1993 (CEC, 1994b).

Overall, arguably the greatest weakness of the system is the lack of genuine independence of the Commission. In its assessment of State aids, the Commission is required to take account of wider *policy* issues like regional development, research and development and environmental protection. However, it is often *political* factors that count. In large measure, the Member States are to blame for this situation, alternately castigating the Commission for its lack of objectivity and taking advantage of the scope to influence individual decisions. Given the difficulties that the Commission has experienced with regard to controlling aid to many high profile restructuring projects, there is a strong case for advising against greater Commission involvement in large individual awards under regional aid programmes, unless an objectively justifiable method of assessment can be agreed or independence can be secured. The current susceptibility to political pressures is damaging to the credibility and coherence of Community competition policy. Arguably the only solution is for the Member States to find the political will to enable competition issues to be dealt with at arms length from national interests.

Looking forward, Community competition policy faces some significant challenges, in two areas in particular. First its capacity to control competition for mobile investment, especially in the light of non-State aid measures which influence location decisions; and second, with respect to the extension of the State aid rules to central and eastern Europe. These are considered in turn.

An important consequence of the detailed nature of Commission intervention in State aid policies is that it may encourage Member States to seek less transparent mechanisms to support firms, and ones which impact on other areas of Community policy.

The regional policies of the Member States have been subject to considerable Commission scrutiny over the last two decades or so, often involving a highly-prescriptive approach to area designation. The regional aids operated by the Member States mainly take the form of grants and are visible and transparent. There is, in consequence, a degree of exasperation among policymakers at the extent of Commission intervention and a widespread suspicion of the activities of other Member States, especially with respect to taxation and the attraction of foreign investment.

Excessive Commission scrutiny of visible and transparent State aid policies may be counterproductive. A number of Member States already operate tax advantages which directly or indirectly assist mobile investment but which fall outside the State aids rules. (These are considered further in the following chapter.) Continued pressure from the Commission on regional investment aids may encourage the proliferation of such measures as Member States seek instruments that are sheltered from scrutiny under Article 92. Importantly, this comes at a time when a number of Member States are concerned about the effects of tax competition and fiscal degradation. Careful consideration is required to adapt competition policy controls to these demands.

Controlling competitive outbidding for mobile investment has been at the core of Commission attempts to rein-in regional aid policies from the start. Ironically, it can be argued that Commission intervention has contributed to a situation in which the main regional incentives in a number of countries have become *de facto* instruments of FDI attraction and are less geared towards non-mobile domestic firms. The relative visibility and comparability of the regional incentives on offer may even facilitate mobile firms and their advisors in playing-off potential locations against one another. Related, international competition may lead policy-makers to consider what level of assistance will be necessary to bring the project to their country (Raines and Wishlade, 1997).

These tendencies, together with concerns about the high levels of aid paid to capital-intensive projects have, as discussed, resulted in a series of proposals to reduce the absolute values of regional assistance offered. The difficulties involved in finding a formula to achieve such reductions is reflected in the fact that current proposals date back to 1990 and successive revisions to them have not proved workable. Of course, the design of mechanisms to reduce aid levels in the EU is not eased by global competition for FDI and the 'prisoner's dilemma' situation that characterises much incentive award decision making. Given that the EU has by far the most developed mechanism for controlling the use of subsidies among sovereign states, it will be a considerable challenge to ensure that the EU as a whole is not damaged in global competition for mobile projects.

The prospect of eastern enlargement may not only strain the Commission's area designation methodology to its limits but it will also impose significant constraints on the new Member States.

The so-called 'Association countries' have essentially agreed to be bound by the Community State aid rules prior to EU membership, by dint of their signature of the Europe Agreements. For six of these countries, the Commission has recommended that accession negotiations begin, with the intention that the *acquis communautaire* be applied on accession, following a reinforced pre-accession strategy. At present, the Europe Agreements typically accept that the entire territory of the Associate countries be treated as an Article 92(3)(a) area (although this is subject to review) – until recently, within the EU this has generally meant that award maxima of 75 percent of eligible investment could be authorised. In practice, however, this facility is likely to be of limited benefit to these countries, and this for several reasons. First, for the most part, the Association countries are unlikely to have the budgetary capacity to fund aid at these levels, particularly in aid forms that would find favour with the Commission.

Second, the aid forms that are most prevalent in the Association countries are those to which the Commission is most opposed. In Poland, for example, some 70 percent of State aid is estimated to emanate from the Ministry of Finance[21]; this is predominantly in the form of State guarantees for restructuring (which, in the EC, would be subject to case-by-case scrutiny) and a variety of tax deferment and debt forgiveness measures which are unlikely to be accommodated within the Commission's interpretation of transparency. Competition policy impacts will not, however, be limited to regulating intervention which might be perceived simply as keeping old structures in place. Again in Poland, for example, a number of so-called Special Economic Zones (discussed in Chapter 3) designed largely to attract foreign direct investment have been established. Even though the whole of Poland is viewed as an Article 92(3)(a) area, this form of assistance is likely to cause serious compliance problems with the

---

[21] Interview with the Anti-Monopoly Office by the author.

competition rules since aid is partly linked to export performance[22]; a measure of the potency of the Europe Agreement in respect of State aids is that it actually withdraws some of the benefits conferred on transforming economies by the WTO subsidies code[23].

A further aspect of the enlargement challenge concerns the existing Member States and the impact of the competition rules on them. As the Commission recognises (CEC, 1997c): 'Enlargement will also have an impact on regional aid policy: with present rules unchanged, some assisted areas in present Member States could be crowded out as a result of the overall increase in eligible areas, and as a consequence of the mechanical effect of enlargement on average EU per capita GDP.'

The implications of this are important and indicative of the inherent tension between competition and economic 'cohesion' at the national and European levels. In the First Report on Cohesion, the Commission stressed that 'cohesion is concerned with increasing economic growth and new opportunities in the poorer regions...and does not imply a reduction in either growth or jobs for others'. The problem is, however, that the current methodology for approving assisted areas pivots around EU averages; lower averages would reduce or eliminate the scope for regional aid to be approved in many western European regions, without, internally, there being a perception that the situation in these regions had improved. In short, eastern enlargement could reduce the capacity of the poorer regions of western Europe to compete for assistance through the use of financial incentives.

Notwithstanding the shortcomings of Community State aid control and the challenges that face it is important to bear in mind the achievements of the EU approach. At the very least, this provides a regulatory framework, some measure of autonomy for the supervisory body, and procedures for enforcement and sanctions that are backed by provisions for judicial review. All this adds up to a system of controlling subsidies that is unique

---

[22] Support for intra-EU exports have been prohibited from the early days of the Community. The Europe Agreements similarly outlaw State aids that distort or threaten to distort competition between the EU and the signatory country.

[23] The WTO subsidies code enables transforming economies to keep otherwise outlawed export subsidies in place for a transitional period; the Europe Agreement outlaws aid that affects trade with the EU – this would certainly include aid that supports exports to the EU.

in international law and finds no parallel even in individual countries with federal structures; for a Community of fifteen sovereign states, this represents a considerable success in cooperation and policy coordination.

6 Tax Incentives

FIONA WISHLADE

Introduction

Post-war trends in the deregulation of economies and the globalisation of businesses have heightened the potential impact of taxation on international capital flows. As capital becomes increasingly mobile, and regulatory constraints are relaxed, governments must intensify their efforts to attract and retain investment. In the EU, the Single Market programme of liberalisation in a number of key areas such as product standards and public procurement has left direct taxation as one of the few policy areas in which national governments have genuine autonomy.

Tax has been used as a FDI policy instrument in both Western and Eastern Europe. As noted in Chapter 3, tax concessions are commonly used in CEE countries to attract FDI projects and are generally more important than financial incentives as a policy tool. Budgetary problems in CEE have been more acute than in Western Europe, and it may be that policy-makers are attracted to policies favouring foregone revenue rather than securing budget appropriations for financial incentives. In Western Europe, the problems are more complex, given the political pressures to balance revenue raising and industrial competitiveness. National policy-makers must weigh the need to maintain a favourable climate for the attraction of inward investment and the retention of domestic capital against the requirement to raise revenues from personal and corporate taxation. The difficulty of achieving this balancing act has led increased attention to be focused on two issues: first, whether and how taxation influences foreign direct investment decisions; and second, whether and how FDI taxation impacts on government revenues.

The lack of empirical evidence on the impact of taxation of cross-border direct investment in Western Europe led to the establishment of the Ruding Committee to conduct its own survey. In some respect, its findings were ambivalent. It concluded that 'although considerable uncertainty remains regarding the quantitative effects of corporation tax on FDI, there is substantial evidence of non-negligible tax effects on the international location of business investment' (CEC, 1992c). A Commission study later concluded that 'tax is a critical factor to a significant minority of head-office decisions, but not generally of importance to other project types' (CEC, 1993). More recent research on the UK and Germany (Pain and Young, 1996) found that 'there is a significant effect of tax competitiveness on the location of FDI', but that 'it may not be straightforward for governments to influence their national tax competitiveness'.

The evidence on the impact of FDI taxation on national tax rates and revenues is also rather mixed. As Table 6.1 shows, rates of corporation have tended to fall and, to some extent, to converge since the start of the 1980s, which might be taken as some evidence of tax competition.

Table 6.1 Overall corporate tax rates (%) in the EC[1]

	1980	*1985*	*1991*
Belgium	48	45	39
Denmark	37	50	38
Germany	61.7 / 44.3	61.7 / 44.3	57.5 / 45.6
Greece		49	46 (40)[2]
Spain	33	33	35.5
France	50	50	34.2
Ireland	45	50 (10)[3]	43 (10)[3]
Italy	36.3	47.8 / 36	47.8 / 36
Luxembourg	45.5	45.5	39.4
Netherlands	46	42	35
Portugal	51.2 / 44	51.2 / 44	39.6
UK	52	40	34
EC average	46	46.9	40.1

Source: OECD (1991) as quoted in CEC, 1992c.

Notes: [1] Where two rates are given the first is the rate for retentions and the second the rate for distributions. [2] The lower rate applies to firms quoted on the Athens stock exchange. [3] The lower rate applies to the manufacturing industry.

Nevertheless, rates of taxation still vary considerably, from over 50 percent in Germany to just 10 percent in Ireland (in respect of manufacturing). However, as has been pointed out (Thomsen and Woolcock, 1993), it is insufficient simply to compare headline rates without taking account of the level of subsidy provided through tax deductions. The UK, for example, offers a relatively low rate of corporate taxation, but few allowances; in contrast, the German rate is high, but there is a significant number of deductions available.

A further complication when making international comparisons arises from the extent to which governments rely on corporate taxes as a source of revenue. As Table 6.2 shows, this also varies widely. Whilst Luxembourg has consistently raised over 15 percent of taxation from corporate sources, in other countries, such as Denmark, Greece and Ireland, the take is under five percent. What is not shown is the scale of employers' social security contributions which contribute towards the financing of the welfare system. In some countries, these make a significant call on corporate costs so that to focus on corporate taxation rates alone is to take only a partial view of policy competition.

Also of interest are the *trends* in the share of corporation tax in total taxation. Over the period shown, the figures suggest that firms are bearing a increasing proportion of taxation; this is the reverse of the position in the US which has seen the share of corporate taxation in total taxation fall from 15.8 percent in 1965 to 8.5 percent in 1989.

The pattern is much more mixed in the European context; there is no consistent tendency in one direction or the other, even if the European average shows a slight increase. Also notable is the fact that European corporation taxes, measured as a share of GDP, actually increased - from 2.3 percent in 1975 to 3.0 percent in 1989. In the US, the share fell from 3.1 percent to 2.6 percent in the same period, and Canada follows a similar trend. In North America, this pattern, and the tendency for the tax burden to be shifted from corporations to individuals, has attracted growing attention. In response, a number of citizens' groups in the US and Canada have started campaigns to reduce the subsidies and tax concessions given to firms – so-called 'corporate welfare' (Thomas, 1997).

In Western Europe, too, there have been growing concerns about the issue of tax competition between countries and whether this might lead led to 'fiscal degradation'; a related issue is the extent to which the burden of taxation is shifted onto revenue raising mechanisms that might discourage job creation. With respect to fiscal degradation, Chennells and Griffith (1997) found no evidence that 'tax competition is driving rates or revenues to zero'; this was in line with the findings of the Ruding Committee which concluded that there was no evidence of competition between tax regimes resulting in a general erosion of tax levels (CEC, 1992c). Notwithstanding this finding, the Ruding Committee recommended the following as priority areas for Community action:

Table 6.2 Taxes on corporate income as a percentage of total taxation

	1975	1980	1985	1989
Belgium	7.2	5.7	6.4	6.7
Denmark	3.1	3.2	4.9	4.2
Germany	4.5	5.5	6.1	5.5
Greece	3.4	3.8	2.7	4.6
Spain	6.9	5.1	5.2	8.6
France	5.2	5.1	4.5	5.5
Ireland	4.8	4.5	3.2	3.4
Italy	6.3	7.8	9.2	10.1
Luxembourg	15.7	16.5	18.2	17.7
Netherlands	7.7	6.6	7.0	7.7
Portugal	n.a.	n.a.	n.a.	3.9
UK	6.7	8.3	12.6	12.3
EC average	6.5	6.6	7.3	7.5

Source: OECD, 1991.

- the removal of discriminatory and distortive features of countries' tax arrangements that impede cross-border business investment and shareholding;
- the setting of a minimum level for statutory corporation tax rates and common rules for a minimum tax base in order to limit excessive tax competition between Member States for FDI or the taxable profits of multinationals; and
- encouraging maximum transparency of tax incentives granted by Member States to promote investment.

Against this background, this chapter considers first the type and nature of tax advantages offered in Western Europe - focusing on the EU - and second, the issues associated with their control.

The Use of Tax Incentives in the EU

Discussions of tax advantages, concessions or incentives are beset with definitional difficulties. This might be regarded as beyond the scope of this chapter, but some understanding of the issues is central to the development of mechanisms to control tax competition. This is particularly so in the EU because tax advantages that constitute so-called 'State aids' are subject to stringent controls and Commission scrutiny under Articles 92 to 94 of the Treaty; however, tax measures that are not State aids fall outside the Commission's sphere of competence.

In its Fourth Survey on State aid expenditure (CEC, 1995b), the Commission notes that there is a lack of clarity in the discussion of so-called 'tax expenditures'. The Survey takes the OECD concept as a starting point. In its study, the OECD (1996a) identifies a list of forms of tax expenditure. These include:

- *Exemptions*: income excluded from the tax base
- *Allowances*: amounts deducted from gross income to arrive at taxable income
- *Credits*: amounts deducted from tax liability
- *Rate reliefs*: a reduced rate of tax applied to a class of taxpayers or activities
- *Tax deferrals*: a relief which takes the form of a delay in paying tax.

The OECD study notes that:

> Defining a tax expenditure is a classification exercise: dividing the provisions of the tax system into a benchmark or norm and a series of deviations from that norm. In general, the norm includes the rates structure, accounting conventions, the deductibility of compulsory payments, provisions to facilitate administration and those relating to fiscal obligations. Where a tax system deviates from this benchmark, a tax expenditure is said to exist.

This is rather broader than the approach taken by the Commission to the definition of State aids. In particular, and as mentioned in Chapter 5, an important feature of the notion of a State aid is the issue of selectivity: to fall within the scope of Article 92 and the Commission purview, a measure must favour certain undertakings or the production of certain goods.

The narrower concept applicable under Article 92 accounts for the substantial differences in tax expenditures as documented by the OECD and spending on State aids in the form of tax incentives, detailed in the Commission's regular spending surveys. According to the Commission study, tax incentives accounted for 34 percent of State aid to manufacturing in the period 1990-92, or an annual average of MECU 12,860 in the same period. This is very considerably below the expenditures registered in the OECD study. In Belgium, for example, the OECD study records corporate tax expenditures of BF 224,934 million (MECU 5,408) for 1992; according to the Commission, annual average expenditure on tax incentives in Belgium in 1990-92 was MECU 341 – less than seven percent of the OECD figure.

Table 6.3 EC government expenditures on tax incentives (MECU)

	1986-88	*1988-90*	*1990-92*	*1992-94*
Belgium	111	330	341	593
Denmark	0	12	15	9
Germany	4,277	4,763	4,549	4,266
Greece	0	181	197	202
Spain	0	2	2	0
France	654	952	1,396	1,117
Ireland	153	161	75	30
Italy	3,413	4,422	5,451	4,535
Luxembourg	3	0	3	0
Netherlands	325	330	136	101
Portugal	277	18	43	121
UK		130	150	89

Source: CEC (various years)
Note: Figures are given in MECU as annual average in current prices.

A review of the promotional material produced by inward investment agencies in Europe makes clear that governments take a wide view of the characteristics of the national taxation systems that might be attractive to incoming firms. Many of these characteristics may only involve advantages relative to other jurisdictions – lower rates of corporation tax are an obvious example. Other aspects are more complicated; the design and structure of the tax system may create benefits not just in relation to other jurisdictions, but also for particular types of firm, transaction or activity within jurisdictions, though these benefits may not always be intentional.

For example, differences in social security contribution rates have been highlighted in FDI promotion, often with notable success (as when Sabena, the national air carrier of Belgium, recently attempted to shift its administrative headquarters to Luxembourg because of the lower social security rates there). However, little evidence exists to suggest that social security tax rates are explicitly manipulated to attract foreign investment. The attractiveness of a country's tax rates to foreign investors may often be a side-effect of, rather than a motive for, tax policy changes.

Consequently, there are relatively few examples of tax advantages explicitly directed at foreign direct investment projects. As discussed in Chapter 4, the main incentives used to attract mobile investment are regional aids, and, for the most part (in large measure as a consequence of Commission pressure) these take the form of capital grants.

Tax advantages are, however, prominent in some jurisdictions, of which the most important are highlighted below. Probably the most well-known is the reduced corporation tax rate in the *Republic of Ireland*. This aims to encourage firms to invest in Ireland by reducing the rate of corporation tax payable on profits earned from the sale of goods manufactured in Ireland. Corporation tax relief is available throughout the Republic in respect of all manufacturing and certain non-manufacturing activities. The award amounts to a reduction in the standard rate of corporation tax (38 percent) to 10 percent.

Corporation tax relief is available in respect of manufacturing profits earned up to 31 December 2010. The scheme is available throughout the Republic of Ireland, but is only available to manufacturing industries and certain non-manufacturing activities including certain shipping activities, ship repairs, production of fish on a fish farm, the sale of goods on the export market by a special trading house (the goods having been manufactured in Ireland by another company), the cultivation of plants in Ireland by the process of plant biotechnology known as micro-propagation or plant-cloning, the cultivation of mushrooms, certain new operations undertaken in the Shannon Airport Zone, computer services (ie. data processing, software development services and related technical or consultancy services), and design and planning services rendered in Ireland in connection with specified engineering works executed outside the EU. The scheme is only available to companies resident in Ireland, and to Irish branches of non-resident companies. Due to the availability of depreciation allowances on machinery and industrial buildings, the effective rate of corporation tax payable during the initial years of business operation may fall below 10 percent, and even as low as zero, the exact rate depending on the capital intensity and profitability of the project. The cost of the scheme in terms of lost revenue is calculated by Irish authorities to have been approximately Ir£ 748.9 million in 1991-92 (OECD, 1996a).

The reduced rate is not restricted to inward investment or mobile projects, but is widely regarded as being responsible for Ireland's success in attracting mobile investment. Numerous business surveys have identified tax rates as the principal location determinant for multinationals locating in Ireland, especially as a base for exporting into the rest of the EU (Ruane and Görg, 1997). Here, the fiscal incentive is made more attractive for companies based in certain countries by double-taxation agreements, designed to maximise the value of the incentives to foreign-owned companies. Importantly, from the perspective of mechanisms to control tax competition, the reduced rate has not been regarded as a State aid by the European Commission.

Substantial incentives also exist for companies locating and carrying on certain trading operations in the Custom House Docks Area, adjacent to the centre of Dublin. The purpose of these incentives is to encourage the establishment of an International Financial Services Centre engaged in internationally-traded financial activities. In this, the incentives have been largely responsible for attracting a number of administrative operations of multinational financial firms, particularly treasury, fund management and other 'back-office' activities (*The Economist*, 1996b). The incentives include a special 10 percent rate of corporation tax to international financial services; rates relief on new buildings and on buildings which are enlarged or improved; 100 percent capital allowances for commercial development; double rent allowances against trading income; and relief for capital expenditure on rented dwellings. Unlike the reduction in the corporation tax rate for manufacturing, these measures are caught by the State aid rules but have been approved by the Commission; however, the value of the concession is not considered to be quantifiable.

In *Belgium*, special measures operate to attract the head office activities of multinational corporations. These are offered within the context of approved 'coordination centres'. Assistance takes the form of a package of measures available to designated headquarters responsible for providing services of an auxiliary or preparatory nature to companies of the group to which they belong. The group must have an 'international character' involving specified minimum levels of activity outside Belgium. Designated Coordination Centres benefit from a number of tax advantages:

- taxable income is determined on a notional basis, ie. on the basis of its overheads, but excluding personnel costs and financial charges;
- Coordination Centres are exempt from registration tax on capital contributions;
- property (land, buildings, equipment) used by Coordination Centres is exempt from withholding tax; and
- Coordination Centres are exempt from withholding tax on dividends, interest and royalties.

A number of these provisions have important implications for international tax planning. In particular, a Coordination Centre can contribute to a tax-efficient financing structure for a group by acting as a financial centre raising funds locally or internationally and granting loans to group companies. In addition, exchange risks can be avoided by using the Coordination Centre as an intermediary for inter-company transactions; any profit made by the Centre on the management of the currency portfolio would be free of tax. Also, the Centre may develop patents etc. and license them to other group companies. Royalty receipts of the Centre would be free of tax whilst payment would normally be tax deductible in the paying country.

Revenue foregone on notional withholding tax on interest amounted to BF 7.3 billion in 1990 and BF 8.4 billion in 1992; with respect to the taxation of Coordination Centres on fixed income, tax expenditures amounted to BF 28.7 billion and BF 46.1 billion, respectively (OECD, 1996a). In total, these sums are considerably higher than regional incentive expenditure, demonstrating the potential importance accorded to such tax incentives in certain countries as an instrument in attracting foreign investment.

In *the Netherlands,* widely viewed as an attractive tax location, the so-called 'participation exemption' is regarded as one of principal elements of the Dutch Corporation Tax Act. The aim of the exemption is to prevent double taxation if the profits of a subsidiary are distributed to its parent company when both are liable for corporation tax. The main features of the scheme are that all gains from shareholdings are exempted, costs associated with a shareholding are not deductible and losses arising from winding up the corporation are deductible only under certain conditions. The corporation distributing the dividend does not have to pay dividend tax if the distribution of profits falls under the participation exemption enjoyed by the company receiving the dividend.

In addition, multinationals can form a reserve for risks relating to foreign participation and financing activities within the group. Up to 80 percent of the profits arising from the financing activities can be added to the reserve so that such profits are effectively taxed at a rate of around 7 percent. This facility is available on request only and is restricted to firms that are resident in at least four other states or on two different continents; the firm's financing activities must be carried out exclusively in the Netherlands.

In *Portugal*, special provisions operate in the autonomous regions of Madeira and the Azores. In the Azores, assistance takes the form of a package of financial and fiscal incentives which aim to diversify the economy and create employment. Assistance is available to firms of any size and sector locating in the Santa Maria Free Zone.

Under the Madeira free zone scheme, aid may take the form of training grants, investment grants and exemptions from taxes. The aim of the scheme is to encourage investment and employment creation in the Free Zone. Assistance is available to firms of any size and in any sector located in the Madeira Free Zone.

The examples mentioned above (which are by no means exhaustive) have focused on tax advantages which hold implicit or explicit advantages for multinational enterprises. In addition, most EU countries operate a range of tax measures that are ostensibly neutral with regard to the origin of the investment. In *Spain*, for example, a corporation tax reduction for investment is provided in respect of certain types of expenditure. In

France, corporation tax relief is available to firms locating in a designated 'Special Investment Zone'. In *Italy*, an important component of the regional aid package takes the form of tax relief.

The Regulation of Tax Competition in the EU

The regulation of tax incentives in the EU raises a number of key policy and political issues. As discussed in Chapter 5, the Community has a relatively sophisticated mechanism for the control of State aids. However, in order for this to come into play, the tax advantages in question must fall within the scope of Article 92; as will be seen, tax advantages and State aids are far from being synonymous. This, coupled with the growing concerns at fiscal degradation and a perceived shift in the burden of taxation away from corporate capital, has led several Member States to call for curbs on the use of 'unfair' or predatory tax advantages. The final section of this chapter is in two parts. The first considers the extent to which tax advantages are covered by the State aid rules; the second reviews recent moves towards the development of a 'code' on taxation in the EC.

Tax Advantages: When are They State Aids, When are They General Measures?

The review of the definition of a State aid in the previous chapter of this study identified the principal characteristics that have emerged from Commission policy-making and European Court of Justice jurisprudence. The elements of the definition are essentially threefold. An aid can be in any form whatsoever, but in order to be classed as aid a measure must:

• be the consequence of State action or involve State expenditure;
• distort or threaten to distort competition; and
• favour certain undertakings or the production of certain goods.

The interpretation of the last of these elements is crucial in distinguishing between what constitutes a State aid within the meaning of Article 92 and what have come to be known as 'general measures'. Moreover, the need to make the distinction is itself of paramount importance because Article 93 only empowers the Commission to take action against measures that distort competition *to the extent that they constitute State aids*; general measures that distort competition must be addressed through other mechanisms, notably Articles 101 and 102. This is essential in the context of tax incentives since responsibility for direct taxation remains with the Member States, unless measures that contravene Article 92 are developed.

As described earlier, the key element in distinguishing between State aids and general measures is the selectivity of the measure and the extent to which it favours 'certain undertakings or the production of certain goods'.

This discrimination can take place on different levels: it might involve the implicit exclusion or inclusion of certain activities or firms; it might involve active discrimination in favour of some firms within a measure that applies to all; or it might involve indirectly benefiting some firms more than others. This discrimination (or exclusion) can usefully be considered with respect to a number of features:

- administrative discretion;
- spatial coverage;
- sectoral coverage; and
- other eligibility criteria.

(i) Administrative discretion

The existence of administrative discretion typically condemns measures to fall within the scope of Article 92(1). However, this is a difficult area in which to attempt to apply demarcations. For a significant range of measures, especially in the field of taxation, there is no direct policy-maker input into the claiming of benefits by individual firms. An obvious example is depreciation allowances which are simply claimed when firms make their tax returns. At the opposite end of the spectrum, many countries operate highly discretionary regional or research grant schemes where policy-makers control eligibility on a case-by-case basis. In between, however, there are many possible shades or degrees of discretion. In particular, to what extent does authorisation for particular tax status involve administrative discretion? In Belgium, for example, Coordination Centres must be approved by the government in order to benefit from the tax advantages set out in the legislation, but it is unclear to what extent any discretion is involved in allowing or rejecting applications. Elsewhere, tax administrations are frequently prepared to give 'advance rulings' on the tax treatment of particular transactions; to what extent might these involve administrative discretion?

(ii) Spatial discrimination

It is well-established that measures which apply only to certain regions of a Member State are caught by Article 92. Tax and social security exemptions granted on a regional basis have consistently been treated by the Commission as constituting State aid. However, this view is largely based on the assumption that there is a national level of tax or social security contribution and that certain areas benefit from a departure from that 'benchmark'. In practice, this involves taking a formalistic view of definitional issues. A number of examples can be used to illustrate this point.

First, the internal institutional and constitutional arrangements vary widely between Member States. In Spain, for example, País Vasco and Navarra have greater autonomy than the remainder of the Spanish regions in relation to taxation to the extent that these regions levy some of their own taxes in place of the national taxation system. This can result in different rates of corporation tax in different parts of the country, without there being any departure from the benchmarks simply because the benchmarks are different.

Second, the extent to which regional and local authorities raise taxes, and the relative importance of those taxes in the overall burden on firms varies considerably. In addition, there can be wide regional variations in the tax burden on firms purely as a consequence of the exercise of local tax autonomy. In Germany, for example, the municipalities (*Gemeinden*) levy, amongst other taxes, a municipal trade tax on income. Within broad parameters set by Federal legislation, the *Gemeinden* are free to set the coefficient (the so-called *Hebesatz*) which determines the rate of taxation in the locality. The *Hebesatz* varies from zero (20 municipalities, of which 16 are in the new *Länder*, have opted not to apply the *Hebesatz*) to 515 percent. This means that the effective rate of trade tax on income varies between 5 percent and 25.75 percent. In other words, what firms pay differs widely between different parts of the country. Whilst the *effect* is arguably the same as a regional grant towards running costs, this type of differentiation falls outside the scope of Article 92.

Third, an extension of this point is the extent to which taxation paid should reflect services provided. It could be argued that different rates of local taxation reflect different policy decisions about the level of amenity. As part of the voting constituency, firms in a given locality can vote for local politicians whose views about the level of services required and the costs associated coincide with their own. In practice, this link is at best indirect. In France, for example, rates of local business tax tend to be higher in communities that are primarily residential and involve high social costs; in mainly industrial areas, rates of local business tax tend to be lower simply because there are more businesses to share the burden and fewer social amenities required. As elsewhere, this has led to differentiated levels of central government funding to local authorities to reflect local needs. Moreover, as in most European countries, the bulk of local and regional government resources come in the form of central government transfers or block grants, diluting the link between the level of tax paid and the services received in return.

(iii) Sectoral discrimination

The issue of sectoral discrimination raises some important questions. For the purposes of the discussion that follows, the key issue is: *in what circumstances does differentiated treatment of specific sectors not constitute an aid?*

A number of countries operate separate taxation regimes for the banking and insurance sectors; these would not normally constitute State aid. For the most part, the Commission considers that differentiated treatment is justified by the special nature of the activities involved and the fact that separate regimes effectively 'normalise' the tax treatment of sectors that would be inappropriately disadvantaged by the application of the general system.

Similarly, the levying of special taxes on particular sectors can be considered part of the general tax system. In the UK for example, oil production is subject to an additional form of corporation tax; it would clearly be absurd if all other sectors of UK industry were deemed to be recipients of State aid because they were *not* subject to petroleum revenue tax! On the other hand, this example does raise the benchmark issue once more; it seems certain that if oil production were to be exempted from corporation tax, then this would be regarded as a sectoral aid - what then is the norm?

The difficulties in identifying the norm are most amply illustrated in the context of the reduced rate of corporation tax applicable to manufacturing industry in Ireland. As mentioned earlier, this is apparently not considered to constitute an aid by the Commission, but rather is viewed to be a part of the general fiscal system, despite its clear importance to incoming investors as a location determinant; it is, however, known that this view is not shared by all directorates in the Commission.

The basic premise for not considering the reduced rate of corporation tax for manufacturing as an aid appears to be the breadth of the sector concerned (and the fact that the rate applies nationwide); were the rate only to apply to parts of Ireland, then it would certainly be viewed as constituting aid - this is confirmed by Commission treatment of the 10 percent rate to international service firms which is restricted to particular centres as well as a closely-defined sector of activity.

In considering the Commission view that the reduced rate is not an aid, it is useful to consider what are the characteristics of the manufacturing sector that merit a lower rate of taxation being applied to it than all other activities. Is the different rate seeking to address an anomaly that would arise from the application of the standard rate? As mentioned above, this is usually the case with the special rules applicable to banking and insurance, but it is difficult to justify with respect to manufacturing.

A related consideration is the *effect* of the measure. The Commission and Court have argued consistently that it is not the *form* of the measure but its *effect* which are key in establishing whether a measure constitutes State aid. It is widely recognised that the reduced rate of corporation tax is a major factor in international location decisions and has been key in attracting industry to Ireland. To ignore this is to take only a partial view of the measure.

It is also useful to take a wider view of how manufacturing is treated for corporation tax purposes elsewhere in Europe. The 10 percent rate is very substantially below the norm for corporation tax rates generally and other countries do not distinguish between manufacturing as against other activities in setting tax rates. This is not to argue that national policy design should be constrained by the policies operated in other Member States, but a consideration of the wider context can help a view to be formed on the justification for the measure; in this case it can be argued that there is no justification for the reduced rate other than the attraction of mobile investment.

(iv) Other eligibility criteria

As the discussion above has shown, the EU Member States operate a considerable number of tax advantages designed to favour particular types of investment or activity. Among these, there are a number of tax advantages which have either been regarded as falling outside Article 92(1) or which have not been reviewed at all. In practice, it has frequently proved difficult to establish whether the Commission has reviewed particular measures since it is only relatively recently that decisions not to oppose particular measures have been published systematically.

The Commission's position on so-called general measures is that Article 92(1) of the Treaty does not apply to general measures applicable to all undertakings in a Member State which meet 'objective, non-discriminatory and non-discretionary requirements'.

However, the Commission has also noted that even measures which are objective, non-discriminatory and non-discretionary may ultimately be viewed as State aids. Of particular interest, however, is the fact that the reverse also appears to be true: not all of the measures which the Commission has deemed to be general are in fact objective, non-discriminatory or non-discretionary.

One example of this is Coordination Centre status in Belgium which is viewed as a general measure. Whilst it is true that the criteria are clear and published (in relation to international status, activities, minimum levels of employment, and so on) and application for Coordination Centre status appears to involve authorisation rather than appraisal by policy-makers, a system for which only a few hundred organisations in the Member State can qualify could hardly be described as non-discriminatory.

Also of interest is the extent to which countries operate different tax systems for different categories of firm. In Greece, for example, there are lower tax rates and evidence of measures that are restricted to quoted companies, a feature which effectively eliminates small and medium-sized firms from eligibility. It is unclear to what extent this could be 'objectively justified' if the tax system as a whole were taken into consideration. Nevertheless, it is clear that if a closer examination is undertaken of the extent to which wholly separate tax arrangements exist for different categories of enterprise, then the margins between general measures and State aids begin to blur and the relevance of the distinction itself becomes increasingly questionable. This is reflected in the 1994 Commission Recommendation on the taxation of SMEs[1] which seeks to encourage Member States to adopt tax structures that are more neutral with respect to the legal status of undertakings. Moreover, the Recommendation explicitly recognises that 'the current structure of rates of personal tax and corporation tax distorts competition between enterprises'. More generally, it is of wider significance that the Commission should have to resort to *persuading* Member States on the basis of Article 155 to reform tax structures that disadvantage certain groups but are considered to be part of the benchmark system; were the same measures to take the form of State aids (and the *effect* might be no different), then Commission scope for action would be far greater.

The Relationship between State Aids and 'Unfair' Tax Competition: Towards a New Code?

This chapter has exposed some of the difficulties in attempting to distinguish between State aids and general measures.

The Commission approach purports to be *effects*-based, but in reality general measures of *equivalent* effect to State aids are treated differently. This is because the Commission can only address State aids under Article 92; it cannot use Article 92 to attack general measures which distort competition.

The requirement for measures to favour certain undertakings or the production of certain goods has put considerable emphasis on identifying the 'norm' from which selective measures depart. This quickly becomes problematic as an approach and runs into difficulties when, for example, a sector is particularly broad (as illustrated by the Irish corporation tax rate

---

[1] OJEC No. L 177; 9.7.94.

for manufacturing) or where there is separate treatment of a given sector because of the specific characteristics of that sector.

The emphasis on identifying departures from benchmarks is a product of the combined forces of legal formalism, political imperatives and historical context; it is one that produces decisions that sometimes lack overall policy coherence.

The formalistic approach flows from the fact that the Commission's power to act is based on the Treaty. It has explicit and wide-ranging powers in respect of measures that amount to State aid; however, the Member States retain sovereignty over direct taxation. As such, Member States are free to design tax structures, decide on systems of local taxation, regulate the balance between taxes on capital and on labour and set rates of taxation; all of this falls outside the Commission's authority (see Figure 6.1). It is only if Member States create exceptions within the overall framework that the State aid rules come into play. This means that regional variations in the tax burden that arise as a consequence of regional tax autonomy are *not* caught by Article 92, but regional variations in the tax burden that arise as a consequence of a decision to favour problem regions *do* fall foul of Article 92. Interestingly, no attempt appears to have been made by the Commission to establish just how great regional variations in taxation are; moreover, there is no evidence that the Commission is even concerned at the scale of these variations, preferring to address only those variations that can be classed as State aid.

Related to this, the Commission lacks a legal basis to address general tax measures that are considered 'unfair' but that do not constitute State aid. Recent work by the OECD on fiscal degradation has isolated a number of factors considered relevant to identifying 'unfair' regimes[2]:

- the special tax regime merely results in a shift of activity to the country providing it, without the creation of significant additional activity;
- the tax burden on internationally-mobile tax bases is significantly lower than that on immobile bases;
- the effective level of taxation applied to activities of non-residents is lower than that applying to residents' activities;

---

[2] Quoted in *Tax Competition in the European Union*, Note for the Economic and Policy Committee and the Monetary Committee, Directorate General for Economic and Financial Affairs.

- the tax incentive is large enough to make it a primary factor in the decision on business location;
- there is no time limit on individual benefits under a preferential regime, or no 'sunset' clause for the regime as a whole;
- the regime does not have a justifiable economic objective (eg. the requirement to create a significant number of jobs); and
- taxpayers may be able to negotiate the level of taxation.

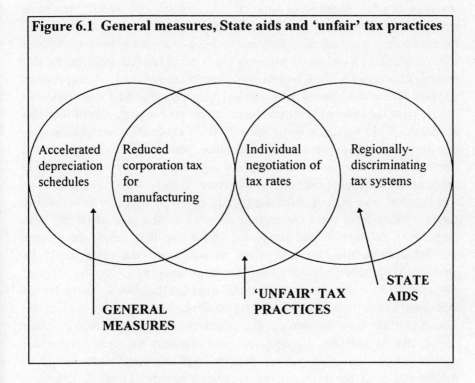

Figure 6.1 General measures, State aids and 'unfair' tax practices

Some of these factors coincide with those that would condemn particular measures to be State aids; however, this is not true of all. Moreover, the converse is true; a regionally-discriminating tax or social security system would not, on the basis of the above listing, appear 'unfair' in an international context, but it is established Commission policy that such measures constitute State aid. In short, the legal formalism of the Treaty means that the Commission's sphere of intervention in addressing measures that distort competition is necessarily partial. This is illustrated in Figure 6.1 which shows that there is no direct correlation between measures classed as State aids by the Commission and those classed as 'unfair' according to the OECD typology.

The political dimension is key. The treatment of taxation under the State aid rules lies at the heart of questions about the relationship between Article 92 and general measures. However, control over the raising of revenues is a key function of national governments and widely viewed as an almost inalienable right. The reluctance of national governments to relinquish any freedom of action in the field of taxation largely explains why progress on fiscal harmonisation has been so limited. Political factors perhaps also underlie the Commission's acceptance of the Irish corporation tax rate for manufacturing as a general measure; for the Commission to dictate what the level of taxation should be for such a large part of the Irish economy would be likely to be viewed as an excessive encroachment on the exclusive competence of the Member States - it is easier for the Commission to take decisions on minor aid schemes than it is to question fundamental aspects of the taxation structure.

Political and legal factors frequently conspire to exclude economic considerations from the Commission analysis. In the context of the Irish corporation tax rate, it was suggested above that there could be a more detailed consideration of the extent to which the reduction could be objectively justified - for example with reference to the special characteristics of the sector or the motivation for the rate. Conversely, for measures which formally *do* amount to State aids (such as regionally-discriminating taxation rates), the Commission could take a wider perspective in reaching its decisions and consider the extent to which similar effects are produced by policies that are outside the scope of Article 92, most notably regional variations in rates of taxation arising from local tax autonomy.

Conclusions

This chapter has sought to assess whether there is tax policy competition for FDI in Western Europe, how that competition manifests itself and how it might be controlled. These are difficult and controversial issues, not least because policy competition is difficult to measure. A possible measure might be the convergence in tax rates that has taken place in the last two decades, but a range of other factors that impact on tax liabilities render this evidence rather weak. A further indicator might be losses of tax revenue brought about as a consequence of tax competition for FDI; recent research has not found evidence of such losses.

Perhaps the most convincing evidence of policy competition and its increase lies in national policy-maker perceptions. As noted in Chapter 5, policy-makers are constrained in their use of financial incentives as an instrument for FDI attraction through the application of the competition rules. As discussed in this chapter, there is a range of significant tax advantages which are implicitly or explicitly targeted at multinational firms, but which fall *outside* the scope of the competition rules. This asymmetry in the scope for control has led some policy-makers to comment that their own administration should contemplate the introduction of such measures as a means of competing for FDI. Publicly, however, the degree of perceived tax competition and concerns at fiscal erosion have led to a growing debate on the need to regulate tax policies. This debate has been fuelled by rising levels of unemployment in many EU countries and considerations of the balance between taxes on capital and labour (in the form of social security contributions). These concerns have been supported by Commission figures suggesting that the implicit tax rate on labour increased from 34.7 percent to 40.5 percent over the period 1980 to 1994, whilst the rate for other factors of production (capital, self-employed labour, energy, natural resources) fell over the same period (CEC, 1996a).

As this chapter has sought to illustrate, the control of tax incentives is beset with difficulties. The identification and definition of what constitutes a tax incentive is problematic, as is what amounts to an 'unfair' or predatory measure. Work by the OECD has provided a starting point for such analysis but the major obstacle to European action and cooperation in this area lies in the nature of taxation as an emblem of national sovereignty and the need to achieve unanimity in Community policy in this sphere.

Notwithstanding this, the Member States and the Commission have begun to make progress towards the establishment of a code intended to curb unfair tax practices. A so-called 'High Level Group' of national tax experts was established in 1996 to consider a range of tax issues, following on from the Commission's 'reflection' document, *Taxation in the European Union* (CEC, 1996b). The Commission subsequently presented a work programme, including a chapter on tax competition (CEC, 1996a).

These developments culminated in the adoption by the Commission of a Communication setting out the broad outlines of a package of measures designed to curb harmful tax competition (CEC, 1997d). This was discussed in late 1997 at a meeting of the Council of Economic and Finance Ministers. The resulting code covers tax measures that have, or may have, a significant impact on the location of business in the EU together with special tax regimes for employees. The criteria for identifying potentially harmful measures are:

- an effective level of taxation that is significantly lower than the general level of taxation in the country concerned;
- the operation of tax benefits that are reserved for non-residents;
- the existence of tax incentives for activities which are isolated from the domestic economy and therefore have no impact on the national tax base;
- the granting of tax advantages even in the absence of any real economic activity;
- that the basis of profits determination for companies in a multinational group departs from internationally accepted rules, in particular those approved by the OECD; and
- lack of transparency.

The proposed code also provides for mechanisms for the exchange and review of information among Member States as well as a 'stand-still' clause involving an undertaking not to introduce new measures which might be harmful to the Community interest. Under the code, existing provisions would later be examined and harmful measures phased out by an agreed date.

It remains to be seen whether such a code will be fully implemented within the Community. Even if it is, its impact may be limited, and this for several reasons. First, initially the code would only apply to proposed new measures; it has apparently been acknowledged that looking at existing measures would result in a clearing house being 'inundated' (*European Voice*, 1997b). Second, the proposed code is voluntary; this means that its effectiveness only lasts as long as the self-interest of the parties to it. Third, and related, the impact of the rules will depend on the effectiveness of the monitoring and enforcement mechanisms. A code based on a 'gentleman's agreement' without an independent policing authority or appropriate sanctions may lack the teeth required to bring Member States tax policies into line.

7 Environmental Policies

KEITH CLEMENT

Introduction

In considering FDI within Europe, a range of factors have been identified as influential both on a company's eventual choice of location and on the relative competitiveness between countries and regions. One element in this range of factors is environmental regulation and policy, the impact of which has been the subject of a number of studies in different areas and at different periods of time. Whereas certain characteristics of this impact are common regardless of location, the European context - because of the proximity of a large number of industrially-advanced, competing economies - has particular distinguishing features, including trends which may be in advance of global changes.

This chapter examines several key determinants of the interaction between FDI and European environmental policies. These comprise the emergence of sustainable development as a framework concept, the relationship of environmental factors to other location factors, the current relevance of the 'industrial flight' hypothesis, the policy competition reflected in European governments' incentives for environmental technology and the growth of the environment industry in Europe.

FDI and Sustainable Development

From a relatively broad notion promoted essentially by public sector agencies, the aspiration of sustainable development has over the past ten years been continually revisited and refined by a wide range of societal and sectoral groupings (Reid, 1995). From its formal launch with the Bruntland Commission Report (World Commission on Environment and Development, 1987), it has been developed by successive public and private sector initiatives, including the Bergen conference in 1990 on Action for a

Common Future, the series of World Industry Conferences on Environmental Management (WICEM), and the United Nations Conference on Environment and Development (UNCED) held in Rio in 1992. A major outcome of the Rio conference was the document Agenda 21, which is a programme of action to press for sustainable development worldwide into the 21st century. Since its launch, Agenda 21 has been supplemented by a series of national sustainable development strategies with European countries and local versions of Agenda 21, which involve partnerships at local level.

In parallel, the International Chamber of Commerce (ICC) has produced its Business Charter for Sustainable Development, launched at the Second World Industry Conference on Environmental Management in Rotterdam. The aims of the Charter include committing enterprises to improving environmental performance and demonstrating to governments and societies that businesses take their environmental responsibilities seriously. Since its launch, the ICC Charter has gained a prominent position and considerable support world-wide, having been signed by over 1,000 companies and associations in 50 countries, with virtually all economic sectors being represented.

All of these have acted as significant influences on European environmental policy-making. Another key initiative with a specifically European context is the series of EU Environmental Action Programmes. The current Programme is the fifth in the series, and it is seen as a significant step in developing a long-term strategy for sustainable development. Unlike previous programmes, it does not rely on directives or regulations, but it seeks to change values towards the environment. Manufacturing industry is one its five key target sectors - also the one that has made most progress, quickly recognising the economic benefits - and international competition is one of the programme priorities.

There is also increasing strategic awareness of environment in the Community's Structural Funds, the regional policy package aimed at the EU's disadvantaged regions and which attracts one-third of the EU budget. Development programmes which may co-finance inward investment must now appraise the existing environment and estimate the likely impact of programme implementation (Clement and Bachtler, 1997).

Other practical steps towards sustainable development in Europe have included the use of environmental management systems especially through the EU's Eco-Management and Auditing Scheme (EMAS), which compares with the International Standards Organisation 14000 series. In practice, Germany has consistently led in the number of EMAS registrations in Europe, with 516 of the 713 EMAS-registered sites. Interestingly, companies have periodically cited public relations and company image in the marketplace as the primary reason for adopting such schemes. Environmental reporting by European industry has also increased in recent years, with two distinct styles of practice still emerging, currently defined as 'Anglo-American' and 'Teutonic' models of reporting (*The Economist*, 1993).

Taken together, these diverse factors represent a broad expansion both in environmental awareness and industrial practice in Europe. The momentum launched and sustained by European governments - national and supranational - has seen a parallel response, mostly by large industry, and the private sector has incrementally moved towards improving environmental performance (Vaughan *et al*, 1997). As this degree of awareness heightens, so does competition between companies and countries. Companies resident in Europe respond to this change partly to match competitors strategies and to retain market share; companies newly entering Europe must be cognisant of this environmental emphasis, and this impacts on business strategy and decision-making and on the corresponding attempts by governments to attract investment.

International Plant Location Factors

As discussed in Chapter 2, a wide range of plant location factors influence investment decisions. Interest in this area has been generated by different countries seeking to understand which factors most attract foreign investment. For example, local and regional development organisations may, through this research, identify areas that need improvement or strengths that should be emphasised in promoting regions to prospective investors. Different studies have placed varying emphasis on the importance of environmental factors.

A major study was carried out in the late-1970s for firms moving into the US (Tong and Walter, 1980). Using a five-point scale, ranging from not important to extremely important, respondents had to indicate the relative importance of 32 plant location factors. The factors were derived from a review of literature concerning foreign investment and location theory, and the researchers used a postal survey method that secured usable responses from 254 companies. In the mean ratings and ranking of these factors, 'climate' appears as number 26 on the list - a relatively passive reference to environment - but otherwise none were related to any aspect of environmental policy (whether legislation, regulation or policy). Around 1980, therefore, environmental regulation (at least in the US) did not feature highly as an international location factor in the research literature nor was it identified as such by foreign investors.

Drawing on more recent work, studies of the anticipated impact of the Single European Market on foreign investment were carried out for the UK's Department of Trade and Industry in 1990 (Bachtler and Clement, 1990a and 1990b). Factors considered relevant for the research included UK and European markets, competitor strategies, workforce skills, infrastructure, economic costs, financial subsidies and language. The environment was not cited as a relevant location factor in the research design, but nevertheless, environmental information did surface in connection with the relative attractiveness of the different European countries. In particular, some chemicals firms cited Spain as a destination, the reason being that the environmental regulatory framework was less developed and implementation was poor. This provided some evidence that environmental policy was exerting an influence in certain polluting sectors.

Subsequent research by Tufts University identified environmental legislation as a significant factor for American companies with European bases (Flaherty and Rappaport, 1991). In a survey of US multinational corporations, 45 of which had manufacturing operations in Europe, Community and national regulation was perceived as the most important aspect of their environmental concern, followed by customer and community opinion. Of course, this approach cannot allow for or even acknowledge that there is variation between countries in Europe and even between regions within countries, but it does suggest an increasing recognition of the need for awareness of legal environmental obligations by companies focusing on new or expanded European investment.

Acquisition forms another aspect of FDI in which environmental issues are becoming more apparent. A study of the environmental strategies, management policies and perceptions in industry indicated that most firms do evaluate the environmental performance of potential partners (Deloitte *et al*, 1990). However, this is generally understood to happen only after the strategic financial and business decisions are made.

The Industrial Flight Hypothesis Revisited

Given that environmental issues appear to be increasing in importance and strategic awareness, potentially rising up the table of international location factors, it is worth considering whether the theory first advanced as the Industrial Flight Hypothesis may have new significance.

The Industrial Flight Hypothesis first became an issue in the late-1970s, when it was argued that US pollution control laws were so severe that they could result in a massive relocation of major manufacturing industry out of the US in order to avoid high costs (as reviewed in OECD, 1997b). The argument was made that as polluting industries came under more regulation, industrial processes would not be improved, only exported - ie. they would stay just as polluting or hazardous, but be based in poorly-regulated countries. US pollution control costs were described as higher than anywhere else, and US industry was described as spending on average twice as much for air and water pollution control as a percentage of capital spending. The problem companies were identified as those with older facilities which could not be made safe just by adding control devices - ie. they needed to be redesigned and rebuilt.

However, the hypothesis was criticised soon after as being based on only a few industries, and no examples were found of industries closing and moving because of high regulatory costs. Moreover, the original research had made no review of foreign direct investment statistics: when examined, these statistics revealed that US outward investment was going to highly-regulated countries, not to poorly-regulated ones; and at the same time, foreign investment was still increasing in the US. The conclusion was that there were no grounds for arguing that over-regulation was driving certain industries out of the US (Levenstein and Ellers, 1980).

To confirm these findings, the United Nations launched a survey on 'environmental aspects of the activities of transnational corporations'. Referring to the ultimate destinations as 'pollution havens', the flight argument was dismissed as based on incomplete reasoning and a number of misunderstandings (UN CTC, 1985). Three main reasons were produced in support of this conclusion:

- environmental differentials cannot be considered in isolation: their significance must be considered within the complete structure of costs, risks and returns which make up location decisions;
- rather than resort to alternative foreign locations, firms prefer to expand at present sites or make internal shifts within countries; and
- pollution-haven investments actually involve much higher degrees of risk - eg. in some developing countries, there are distinct anti-multinational sentiments, and this presents a potentially bad investment climate, often in addition to unstable governments. For export-oriented investments, there would be large transport costs in getting the product to the market (as supporting infrastructure is often lacking) so that plant construction and bringing in qualified management may present higher costs than in the home countries.

Overall, the UN found very little evidence of foreign investment being seriously influenced by environmental factors. There had been a number of cases of firms being blocked domestically on environmental criteria, and so they had looked for foreign alternatives; however, this was not a major shift. Following this report, it became fashionable to describe the notion of polluting industry fleeing abroad as a myth.

Within the European context, a study in 1979 revealed German firms as not significantly influenced by environmental costs (as reported in Clement, 1994a). They wanted to stay near the market, and preferred to meet higher environmental costs at home rather than relocate to developing countries. Instead of moving, they tended to develop better technologies for their products in industrialised countries, and usually later installed these technologies in developing countries, anticipating higher environmental standards being introduced there eventually. In spite of these realities, the German firms admitted that they still threatened their government with relocation when negotiating siting decisions.

A similar example comes from the Netherlands in the last decade, where a major Dutch chemical company threatened to leave Holland unless environmental concessions were made by the authorities (Clement, 1993). If the concessions were not forthcoming, the company stated its intention of moving just across the border to Belgium. When the Dutch government refused to concede, there were no further developments - the company had been bluffing, but it would have readily accepted relaxed regulations.

A good example of a European country which has been targeted for environmental reasons is Ireland, a country that receives more FDI than its economic size would suggest (Leonard, 1988). In the 1970s, the Irish Industrial Development Authority (IDA) decided to tackle unemployment by attracting international chemicals companies. These were so-called 'dirty industries', but they had significant job creation potential, so there was an initial willingness to sanction their introduction into Ireland. Rather than see the workforce departing for the pollution of London, they preferred to import the pollution and keep people in Ireland. The strategy was also defended on the basis that Ireland had a high environmental assimilative capacity - the ability of the natural environment to absorb and dispose of pollutants - especially due to the frequent rainfall and high wind speeds. Behind the scenes, IDA officials were paving the way for these industries, holding meetings with environmental authorities to ensure their cooperation: for the benefit of the economy, they were negotiating less stringent pollution control. American chemicals firms were the main beneficiaries of these deals, and which were subsequently described as 'permission to pollute', following a case in which there was substantial dumping of untreated waste in Cork Harbour.

The IDA was severely criticised for this strategy in later years, and it has since adopted a new strategy that includes environmental impact assessment and choosing sites to minimise environmental impact. The development of the new strategy was made easier because of the success of the IDA's inward investment drive. This now brought in a range of industries, including healthcare and fine chemicals, and it meant they could now be selective, so that there was no great need to pursue heavy chemicals investment. Public pressure was also a factor, as a momentum was building up for environmental protection and more sensitive project selection.

At present, the attitude to using environmental policy as a means of both rejecting and attracting polluting industry in Europe is very different. The notion of an ecology-growth trade-off - in which governments calculate the economic benefits of inviting environmental damage - is being replaced by one of the inevitable progress towards sustainable development in which environmental issues are becoming more important as a location factor. In this revised scenario, environment features not as a negative but as a positive incentive.

With the new environmental awareness, the growth (and anticipated further growth) in the environment industry and the increase in private sector jobs with designations such as Environmental Manager, the new hypothesis to be verified is no longer industrial flight but industrial attraction through environmental criteria (OECD, 1996b). Current competitive drives to promote European locations as destinations for investment identify environmental advantages ranging from the quality of life and proximity to attractive landscapes through to clear business advantages of being located in a country or region with high environmental standards and strict regulations. The latter can include: credentials such as eco-audit and eco-labelling registrations being presented as business catalysts; recycling and energy efficiency being shown to bring financial benefits; and supply chain linkages characterised by supplier and customer environmental audits which go beyond minimum compliance to be in advance of legislation or ahead of targets.

Incentives for Environmental Technology in Europe

Within this new framework of countries seeking to encourage good environmental practices and improved environmental performance, 'clean' technology is a key factor in facilitating the effective transition to sustainable production (Clement, 1994b). Accordingly, this section examines the support offered by European governments for environmental technology . Whereas these financial instruments are generally available to indigenous and incoming industry - and as yet, they would not be expected to present a competitive attraction on their own - they do form a component of FDI deals and packages, and this component is expected to increase in future years, potentially generating significant elements of policy competition.

In instances where strict regulation promotes the use of cleaner technologies or more resource-efficient methods, some European governments have responded by providing subsidies to help firms make practical moves towards sustainable production. Although the utilisation of subsidies to cushion the impact of regulation is criticised as inappropriate in the context of the Single Market, the counter-argument advanced is that firms that can be persuaded to invest early can realise advantages of efficiency and productivity; in practice, those countries with the toughest environmental regulations are in fact the largest exporters of environmental technologies and services (Stevens, 1992).

Periodic surveys from the European Commission monitor both social and economic cohesion and progress towards the Single Market. Within these surveys, statistics on total State aid to EU manufacturing show considerable variation between countries, although the major investors in industry are identified as France, Germany, Italy, Spain and the UK (CEC, various years). In terms of the objectives of the assistance, a different order of significance prevails when environment is considered (Table 7.1). Although the surveys should be treated with caution, as there are problems in classifying aid schemes by objective (a scheme with direct environmental aims may be considered under other business scheme headings), they do illustrate differences within Europe. From its leading position on total aid to manufacturing, Italy fails to register environmental expenditure, and Germany moves to the front position, with the UK in second place with 40 percent of the German total.

If environmental assistance is then considered as a percentage of manufacturing assistance (Table 7.1), another scenario places Denmark as the most committed, with four percent of its manufacturing aid dedicated to environmental schemes. In second place, three countries are equal, as Germany, the Netherlands and the UK each registered two percent.

Of the environmental schemes available to industry investing in Europe, the majority have a technology component. The current distribution between Member States comprises eleven in Germany, nine in France, three in each of Belgium and the Netherlands, two in each of Denmark and Luxembourg, and one in each of Greece, Italy, Spain and the Netherlands (Clement, 1997). In terms of subject matter, these incentives range from general environmental protection and environmentally-friendly investment to specific research and technology applications.

Table 7.1 Environmental expenditure in the Community, 1981-90 [1]

	1981-86		1986-88		1988-90	
	Total (MECU)	% of total aid [2]	Total (MECU)	% of total aid [2]	Total (MECU)	% of total aid [2]
Belgium	0	0	0	0	0	0
Denmark	7	1	8	4	14	4
Germany	92	0	103	1	162	2
Spain	0	0	6	0	16	1
Greece	0	0	0	0	0.5	0
France	6	0	27	1	28	0
Ireland	0	0	0	0	0	0
Italy	0	0	0	0	0	0
Luxembourg	0	0	0	0	0.5	1
Netherlands	27	3	17	2	30	2
Portugal	0	0	0	0	0	0
UK	-	-	16	1	64	2

Source: CEC, various years.

[1] - For some countries, environmental expenditure may come under other business scheme headings. [2] - Share of environmental expenditure of total State aid to the manufacturing sector.

The principle forms of the incentives are grants, soft loans (offered at below market rates of interest or with 'repayment holidays') and tax relief through accelerated depreciation allowances. In some cases, a scheme may be offered in more than one of these forms, depending upon the type of project being considered for support. Grants dominate the environmental technology schemes, accounting for 60 percent of the assistance available; soft loans comprise 30 percent of the total; and special depreciation allowances account for the remaining 10 percent. Two of the grants have an interest subsidy option (in Belgium and Luxembourg).

With regards to targets or aspects of environmental technology actually funded by the schemes, the emphasis is on investment (often with associated training). This accounts for 40 percent of the measures available. In comparison, 30 percent of the schemes are aimed at research and development; 20 percent support demonstration of pilot projects; and 10 percent relate to feasibility studies. Interestingly, one-fifth of the environmental technology incentives have an SME clause - ie. small and medium-sized firms are given preference, higher rates of award or exclusive access. This is sometimes linked to location, with all firms being eligible in enterprise zones, but only SMEs outside these zones.

Considering the impact of these financial incentives on European FDI, it is generally believed that, unless the sums involved are very substantial, the impact is not decisive (as described in Chapter 4). In other words, inward investors often regard these one-off or fixed-term financial inducements as windfall gains, and they are usually secondary to other factors such as market proximity, availability of a skilled workforce and competitors' strategy. Nevertheless, within that hierarchy, it is likely that environmental incentives will increase in status as international industry orients itself more towards the priorities of the next century.

Even though governments may ultimately find environmental technology incentives useful in attracting investment, in a broader perspective this does not appear to be an effective means of tackling environmental problems. In the Tufts survey cited above, technological limitations were perceived as the least significant obstacle to environmental progress (Flaherty and Rappaport, 1991). Instead, institutional and managerial barriers were considered as more substantial, implying that improved environmental practices are more likely to arise from better management rather than better technology, or indeed from an effective combination of both of these concerns (Ashford, 1993).

Environmental Factors in Central and Eastern Europe

In focusing attention on Central and Eastern Europe as an investment location, the European Commission held a conference in Budapest in 1991 on 'environment, industry and investment decisions'. Organised by DGXI, the Environment Directorate, the conference addressed the three issues of: (i) environmental evaluation, assessment and management; (ii) financial investment; and (iii) the environmental impact of privatisation. Its conclusions were that the political and economic restructuring in CEE offered considerable scope to improve environmental practices; and that this presented a useful opportunity to promote production and consumption based on sustainable development principles. Whereas the legislative and administrative frameworks in CEE could not yet effectively protect the environment, incoming investors were encouraged to operate or build to standards they would expect in their home countries. As a basis for action, the conference produced guiding principles, intended to supplement existing charters or codes of practice such as the ICC Business Charter for Sustainable Development.

Nevertheless, foreign investors in CEE can still expect a number of problems and uncertainties environmentally (Barrett *et al*, 1993). For setting-up projects or greenfield investors, these problems might include proximity to major polluters or environmental hazards, contaminated land, the costs of water treatment and air clean up before production (to protect products), and coping with higher environmental standards than existing industry. In addition, there is differentiation in how foreign investors are treated. They may be seen as a valuable source of income, and so receive preferential treatment or even environmental regulatory exemptions; alternatively, they may be faced with less flexibility, and they could even be made an example of, with very strict treatment.

Those investors entering CEE through joint ventures can face slightly different problems: the upgrading of antiquated plant to meet regulations, fines for non-compliance, the expense of importing pollution control technology, the expense of training staff, liability for staff health, and the problem of repatriating profits. In this case, the unknown factor would be whether they might possibly avoid the potentially strict controls on foreign investors.

Investment in CEE is one area which clearly prompts a different assessment of priorities amongst business, as environmental issues rise in importance relative to factors such as unstable economic reforms, business risks, legal and administrative uncertainties and exchange rate risks (World Bank and OECD, 1992). Business surveys have also revealed that, for the majority of Western investors in CEE, environmental issues can be a significant impediment, with the consequence that investment is frequently delayed until environmental liability is quantified and allocated equitably - so side-stepping attempts by CEE governments to take on the costs of clean-up.

Part of the problem relates to earlier experiences, when deals closed with no environmental audits and only vague provisions on liability. Even in joint ventures, major companies have had media and public relations problems with liability for pollution created some 20 years ago (Manser, 1993). However, CEE governments are increasingly encouraging audits to set an environmental baseline, and a new development is that environmental clean-ups are beginning to be negotiated in advance. The pressure is on companies to investigate environmental liabilities, bearing mind that if a CEE government insists on Western environmental standards - such as Dutch safeguards - these may prove too expensive for implementation and ultimately could discourage the investment altogether.

In overview, the investment opportunities presented by the CEE countries bring with them a serious environmental legacy. Although the Western European economies have parallel duty-of-care responsibilities, the extent of degradation is much greater in CEE, and the additional problems such as failures of communication between environment and privatisation ministries further hinders the realisation of FDI. With regards to future comparability, the CEE countries are reviewing their environmental legislation with a view to ensuring strict regulation and implementing identical standards across Europe, especially those countries seeking early membership of the EU. Interestingly, the view in CEE is not that tough environmental regulation deters investment, but rather that it increases compliance and filters out inappropriate investment.

Conclusions

Research into environmental factors and inward investment has produced differing perceptions over time. Formerly, most researchers in this field were of the opinion that environmental policy does have some impact on European FDI decisions; however, the point where they differed was in the degree of that impact. The common view has been that the impact is small, statistically insignificant, and with more of a micro rather than macro relevance - ie. for specific firms or sub-sectors, where environmental costs are proportionately higher, rather than for whole industries.

With progressive moves towards sustainable development - nationally, internationally and globally - a new perspective has replaced former preoccupations with regards to the environment, bringing in a positive dimension which constructively lends itself to the generation of competition. Conventional thinking previously suggested that this competition was determined by how rigorously environmental regulation is enforced; in other words, competition could arise through the covert lowering of standards. This is now less common, and it can be expected to continue to diminish in the context of high, uniform EU standards and increasing moves towards harmonisation.

Where policy competition between countries may focus more in future is in the raising of standards or the active promotion of the advantages of existing high standards. This is linked to notions of offering incoming firms a positive image, good public relations, resource efficiency in production, and leading-edge positioning amongst trends in international competition. The high standards of the new EU Member States (Austria, Finland and Sweden) and the associated transitional environmental agreement which supports their accession gives further impetus to the likelihood that a proactive orientation towards environment will remain an EU characteristic. In this scenario, within individual Member States or regions, high-profile competition to attract industry into areas well above minimum environmental standards could regularly feature in inward investors' assessment of critical location factors.

Accordingly, with regards to the impact of environmental factors on FDI, future European influences are more likely to be on the destination rather than the overall volume of new investment. From earlier visions of flight *out* of highly-regulated countries, the new reality may encompass a flight *into* highly-regulated countries. With some governments now moving towards more participatory regulatory regimes, the matching corporate response is to work with governments rather than against them. This has been some years in its development as a philosophy, but the direct benefits and the new public-private sector balance which will result may ultimately lead to the realisation of a new and much more effective means of preventing pollution.

8   Labour Market Regulation

PHILIP RAINES

Introduction

Labour market factors have traditionally exerted a significant - if not primary - influence on the location of investment within Western Europe. As key factors of production, differentials in wage levels and the availability of skilled labour have been sufficiently wide in Europe to affect location decisions, as is regularly attested in business surveys on FDI determinants (Ernst & Young, 1995; CEC, 1993). From a policy perspective though, there has traditionally been little scope for governments to influence these labour market factors in order to enhance a region's attractiveness. In theory, labour costs can be affected by the level of non-wage social protection charges set for companies, but while Western European countries have shown wide variation in how high these costs can be, they have not fundamentally altered the *relative* ranking of countries (Adnett, 1996). Similarly, although the supply of skilled labour in a region is dependent on the mixture of education and training measures adopted at national and regional levels, governments have not set their policies with the specific intention of attracting foreign investment. Where training subsidies are used as part of financial packages for foreign investors, they tend to be included as 'sweeteners' by local and regional authorities rather than form the main incentives (Raines and Wishlade, 1997).

In recent years, policy has developed a more significant role as other labour market factors have emerged as location determinants. In particular, corporate restructuring has increasingly taken account of the ability of companies to organise their production and working arrangements. The pressures of globalisation in several industries have prompted companies to maximise the flexibility of their manufacturing and distribution systems, both externally (though the use of just-in-time procedures and close links with local suppliers) as well as within plants (with the new emphasis on flexible working time and team-based approaches). As employment conditions consequently become a greater area of concern to companies, investment decisions are more sensitive to differences in national regulatory environments. For example, in a report by UNICE (1995), employment law was listed by companies as second to taxation as the major constraint on their business activities.

Within the EU, the most visible policy implication of this has been the debate over the Social Chapter. As part of the attempt in the Maastricht Treaty negotiations to extend Community competency to a wider range of social and labour market issues, the Social Chapter was originally envisaged as a natural accompaniment to the deregulatory programme of completing the Single Market. By removing the remaining trading barriers within the Community, one of the main aims of the Single Market programme was to catalyse restructuring in several European industries in order to increase their global competitiveness. At the same time, European policy-makers were cognisant of the dangers of restructuring creating downward pressures on Member State social and employment conditions, and so the Social Chapter was partly designed to act as a bulwark against competitive bidding in labour market standards between countries (Adnett, 1996).

In addressing these issues, the following chapter examines the role of labour market regulation in attracting FDI from several perspectives. It begins with a review of the theoretical issues, particularly the controversy surrounding 'social dumping' within Western Europe and the importance of labour market flexibility. The second section considers the evidence for the impact of different regulatory environments on different types of investment. In the third section, the extent to which this has resulted in policy competition between Western European countries is discussed, as well as the efforts within the EU to limit that competition, and lastly, the chapter's conclusions are presented.

Labour Market Regulation and Foreign Investment: Theoretical Considerations

Before proceeding, it is important to provide a definition of labour market regulation. One provided by Grubb and Wells (1993) argued that:

regulation exists when an individual employer cannot, even by agreement with his or her own employees, use particular working arrangements or forms of employment contract, without risking legal sanctions or the invalidity of the relevant provisions in the contract.

This definition of 'working arrangements' can be widened to include a range of issues associated with working conditions and the scope for employees to negotiate - or be informed of - any alteration to either those conditions or the provisions of employment contracts. The subject of working conditions introduces the complex issue of health and safety regulations. In recent years, there has been a tendency for employment rights and health and safety issues to overlap at European level, most famously in the introduction of EU employment condition policies as health and safety measures by the European Commission. Nevertheless, health and safety issues will not be covered here, mainly because sectoral differences in the type and importance of specific regulations are too large to discuss in the current context. Hence, labour market regulation will be considered under a series of five headings, relating to different aspects of employment and pay conditions: recruitment and dismissal; atypical work; working time; employee consultation; and bargaining arrangements.

- *Recruitment and dismissal* A substantial part of national labour market regulation is employment protection legislation. Restrictions have existed on the ability of companies to recruit, as some countries oblige employers to use public employment offices which can have a strong influence on workers that can be hired. More importantly, limits have been placed on the freedom, timing and scale of dismissals, the levels of redundancy payments and the mechanisms for ruling on unfair dismissals. In some countries, prior authorisation is required before dismissals can be made, which has led companies to take the costs of dismissals into consideration when setting wage rates. Regulations of mass dismissals are especially important, as they can not only involve statutory protection but also collective agreements between management and unions. Many countries insist on consultation with workers representatives before company action, sometimes requiring firms to present a 'social plan' showing how laid-off workers can be found other jobs.

- *Atypical employment* Increasingly, non-standard employment contracts are becoming popular in certain countries and for certain types of work. For example, in 1991, temporary employment through fixed-term contracts affected approximately one in eleven workers in the EU, an increase in absolute numbers of 34 percent over the previous four years (InfoMISEP, 1994).   Similarly, part-time employment is particularly important in many service sectors, such as retailing. Regulation can determine not only the extent to which employers can make use of these different contractual forms (eg. in avoiding claims of unfair dismissals), but also the costs of their use, mainly through employer liabilities for social security contributions.   Statutory or collective agreement limits have been placed on the number of renewals of fixed-term contracts as well as the maximum duration of all atypical employment for individual workers.   Some countries require companies to consult with unions before introducing atypical work.

- *Working time* Working time issues consist of several areas where national regulation has been influential: length of working week, holiday and leave entitlements, and night shifts. With respect to working week regulations, restrictions on the maximum length of working week can have a restrictive impact on employment in certain sectors and economic activities. Regulations also often govern the entitlements to employees of paid holiday time as well as parental leave.   Where regulations affect the pay and conditions of workers on night shifts, these can affect the business costs of maximising plant capacity for production.

- *Employee consultation* In many companies, workers' councils exist to provide employees with a channel for information on important changes in corporate strategies and, in some cases, allowing workers to take part in strategy-making (though usually in a limited capacity). National regulations have differed over the requirement for employee representation, and the powers and responsibilities of workers' councils.

- *Bargaining arrangements* Industrial relations institutions place important limits on the ability of companies to alter unilaterally pay and employment conditions. The institutional backgrounds of EU countries can differ considerably, both in terms of the extent of unionisation in the national labour force as well as in the degree of centralisation and coordination in negotiations over pay and employment conditions. In this context, what is important to businesses is the level at which wage and employment issues are decided and the resulting autonomy for individual companies to negotiate plant-specific agreements.

In recent years, the debate over the appropriate levels of employment regulation in an economy has been linked to the issue of labour market flexibility. This can be viewed as the ability of firms to adapt the organisation of production to existing and anticipated changes in markets, products and production processes. Labour market regulation has a central role in the development of flexibility, both in limiting it where flexibility is seen as unacceptably damaging to the welfare and rights of employees as well as in encouraging it where flexibility can assist in overall job creation.

The pressure to enhance, and the opportunities to achieve, greater flexibility within firms has arisen because of greater competition in many product and services markets. With the increasing internationalisation of sectors in the EU following the Single Market programme, companies have been given incentives to become more responsive to market changes, both in terms of volume as well as of product developments. In several manufacturing industries, production systems have adapted to the need for faster market response through just-in-time working practices in order to cut down inventories and delivery times. These processes have highlighted two different types of flexibility: *external* and *internal*.

External, or numerical, flexibility can be defined as the employers' ability to alter the overall size of the production unit, especially in employment terms. From the perspective of firms, expansions and reductions in the workforce tend to be made in response to significant changes in output (resulting from market trends) and changes in the relative cost of capital and labour (because of relative variations in these costs and developments in production technology). Flexibility can take place within the 'core' (usually full-time) workforce through the latitude and costs of firms in taking on and shedding labour. It can also influence the cost of maintaining a 'peripheral' labour force, which includes the use of 'atypical' (temporary and part-time) employment on non-core business activities or tasks in which there is relatively low transaction costs involved in high personnel turnover. The use of atypical employment by employers is often viewed as less costly than full-time employment because of the reduced exposure to employer contributions for social protection. Extending the argument further, many companies have decentralised their production by sub-contracting more of their business activities to external firms, consequently shifting out the burden - and cost - of adapting to market changes.

Internal flexibility reflects the capacity of firms to change the working arrangements of their existing labour force rather than its overall size, notably with respect to temporal and functional flexibility.

* *Temporal flexibility* Working time has become a more important aspect of flexibility for several reasons. Partly there is a direct cost element to the issue, as longer hours worked by employees can theoretically reduce the costs of taking on new people and training them to take over the tasks. However, to a large extent it is a response to the increasing need for firms either to maximise production output through continuous plant operation or to reduce and expand output in markets characterised by significant variation (such as the retail sector, where shopping demand changes at different times of year). Temporal flexibility includes not only the number of hours worked in a certain period of time (where adjustment can take place through overtime or shorter working weeks) but also the arrangements for working time within a period, such as shift work and flexitime.

* *Functional flexibility* With regard to task allocation, some employers have found that the ability to reassign workers quickly and smoothly to different tasks can increase productivity. It may be important to have a labour force that can adapt efficiently to changes in the production system, particularly when short-term bottlenecks occur. Moreover, functional flexibility is necessary where part of the workforce is organised into teams and allocated particular problems to solve, requiring the employees to carry out a range of different tasks. Attempts to deregulate job definitions - through the removal of closed shops and task demarcation as well as by decreasing the number of job pay grades within companies - have aimed to increase the mobility of workers between tasks in the production process.

Companies will aim to maximise these different types of flexibility for the least cost. Where the goal of optimising such flexibility becomes important enough to affect investment location decisions, social dumping may take place as mobile investment is attracted to areas where labour is least protected. Usually, social dumping is understood in the context of competition between countries over labour costs, but with regard to issues of flexibility, there is an additional policy competition element. If governments perceive the regulatory environment to be an important location determinant, pressures will be placed on rival governments to lower their social and employment protection standards in order to attract - and retain - investment.

Social dumping is traditionally regarded as an investment issue between the developed and developing world, where the gap in employment protection levels offers considerable incentives for firms in labour-intensive industries to relocate their production. It has only recently been highlighted as a phenomenon taking place *within* Western Europe (as opposed to between Western Europe and lower cost parts of the world), mainly in response to several recent trends. First, as noted above, flexibility has emerged as an important goal in manufacturing across Europe, so firms have been more sensitive to FDI locations that maximise their production flexibility. Second, as described in more detail below, policy differences among Western European countries widened over much of the last two decades - largely due to the UK Government's intensive dismantling of employment protection legislation in the UK - creating scope for greater policy competition. Lastly, concerns over social dumping have been heightened by restructuring within several industries in the wake of progressive European economic integration. Within the EU, the completion of the Single Market not only catalysed a surge of investment into the Community, but between European countries as well. The role of market proximity factors may have declined in importance, as distribution across national markets from single sites has become easier for some industries with the removal of trade barriers. As a result, production factors are becoming more important in determining investment: labour costs, availability of skills, and the level of employment regulation.

Labour Market Flexibility and Location Decisions: Evidence

Although the issue has been increasingly debated in Western Europe, conclusive evidence for social dumping has been difficult to establish, in large part due to the sensitivity of firms in identifying such factors as significant determinants of their investment decisions and the problems in separating social dumping factors from other determinants. As a result, the debate has tended to focus on a few well-publicised examples.

The most famous of these in recent years was the 1993 decision by Hoover Europe to close down its factory outside Dijon in France and transfer production to its existing plant in Cambuslang in Scotland. What distinguished this relocation was that it appeared to pivot on Scottish workforce concessions over working arrangements, trade union representation and pay, many of which the French workers were unable to make (EIRR, 1993). Although labour cost differentials played a significant role and the Scottish negotiations were not directly aimed at attracting the relocation investment, the Scottish workforce was able agree to a 'no-strike' deal and the exclusion of new employees from the occupational pension scheme for two years, two concessions that the French workers would have been unable to offer. In particular, the case highlighted the ability of Scottish workers to negotiate at plant level whereas in France, workers were to a large extent constrained by wider collective agreements.

The case sparked a fierce wave of accusations by French government ministers against the UK, whose refusal to join the Social Chapter - and its approach to employment deregulation in general - was characterised as a 'beggar-thy-neighbour' policy explicitly aimed at attracting inward investment by removing the legal protection for workers rights. However, in many respects, this is an unusual case, as it deals with a clear example of a relocation based solely on labour market factors - in practice, where direct relocations take place, they are determined by a variety of cost factors. Consequently, such relocations have been relatively rare, so it is worth considering the role of social dumping in other types of investment in Western Europe where a transfer of production is not so explicit, particularly greenfield and expansion investments. The issue here is whether workforce flexibility - and by implication, the regulatory environment - is a significant factor in investment decisions.

In *greenfield* investments, location decisions are usually based on a combination of different factors, making it difficult to isolate overriding determinants. Business surveys suggest that the main factors in Europe have consistently been market proximity (though less dominant than before), labour costs and the availability of skilled workers (CEC, 1993). Labour market regulation has been noted in these surveys, but it is not perceived as a critical influence. Differences in regulatory environments only appear most important in investment in certain countries, notably the UK, where it has been often listed as an key factor (*Financial Times*, 1996c). Anecdotal evidence of companies locating in the UK reinforce the importance of the country's reputation for a flexible labour market, in combination with low labour costs. For example, in its recent huge investment in North East England, Samsung cited the flexibility of the UK workforce, though other factors - including the financial incentives it received - will have been very influential (*The Times*, 1995).

More evidence appears to exist in the case of *re-investments*, though the data on the expansion and contraction of existing sites is sparse. Multinationals in many industries are sensitive to labour market differences in terms of how they invest in different plants across the EU and how they bargain with their labour forces. Increasingly, multinationals have been using their investment strategies to extract concessions from workforces in different plants to increase productivity (Ferner, 1994). The following examples underline the trend.

- Recio (1992) noted that some multinational investors in Spain were using the threat of firing temporary workers and withholding investment plans in their collective bargaining to secure greater numerical flexibility, such as working on Saturdays.

- Mercedes-Benz decided to make a significant production investment in its Untertürkheim plant in Germany rather than in neighbouring Alsace in France (where labour costs were lower) because of the willingness of the German workforce in agreeing to more flexible working time arrangements to maximise machinery operating hours and the introduction of more performance-relatedpay (EIRR, 1994).

- General Motors Europe used differences in productivity in its European plants - resulting from the introduction of more flexible working practices - to put pressure on lesser-performing plants to make concessions on working time arrangements, team-working, use of temporary employment and dispute procedures (Mueller and Purcell, 1992).

It should be pointed out that the negotiations between companies and workforces over more flexible organisation of labour is not necessarily conducted in hostile circumstances. Often, both sides can make concessions to improve productivity, as when Opel in Germany secured a more flexible arrangement of working time to ensure continuous production without increasing the average number of hours worked by employees (*Financial Times*, 1995). Furthermore, the use of investment strategies as a bargaining counter in negotiations over working conditions tends to be limited to certain types of sectors. In some industries, manufacturing investment is linked to particular markets or R&D specialisms that preclude potential investment shifts. Some multinational companies have been organised so that different plants have specialised in their product lines, giving the company very limited scope for moving investment between plants.

Is There Regulatory Competition in Western Europe?

The responsiveness of investment decisions to differences in regulatory environments across Western Europe can be partly explained by the extensive variation in labour market regulation - and consequently, labour flexibility - in Europe. In the table below, a ranking has been made of countries in the EU, utilising work by Grubb and Wells (1993) and a European Commission labour force survey measuring the share of companies which listed recruitment regulations as a barrier to increasing employment (CEC, 1995d). Grubb and Wells ranked countries by ease of dismissal procedures (in terms of notice, severance pay and legal difficulties of dismissal), eligibility of part-time and temporary workers for the same rights as full-time workers, and restrictions of weekly hours and working on weekends and night shifts. The figures are averaged across the different types of flexibility to give a crude, but revealing indication of differences in regulatory environments within the EU.

With some exceptions, flexibility in its different forms is broadly more apparent in some countries more than others. Ireland and the UK (the latter by a notable margin) have the most flexible labour environments, whereas Greece and Portugal may be characterised by having regulations that make external and temporal flexibility more difficult to achieve. In some countries, restrictions in one area of labour market flexibility can have significant effects in another. Hence, the severe restrictions in Spain on employment dismissal have led to the extensive use of temporary employment, so that Spain has the highest share of fixed-term contract workers in its labour force of all EU countries (Sysdem, 1995).

Table 7.1 Labour market flexibility in the EU (1993)

	Numerical flexibility			Temporal flexibility			Av.
	*Recruit-ment**	*Dis-missal*	*Part-time workers*	*Temp-orary workers*	*Limits on hours/ week*	*Week-end/ night shift*	
Belgium	3	4	8	11	10	5	6.8
Denmark	-	2	5	1	11	2	4.2
France	10	5	3	8	7	7	6.5
Germany	5	7	6	9	8	6	6.8
Greece	7	8	9	7	4	10	7.5
Ireland	8	3	1	1	2	3	3.0
Italy	5	9	9	10	6	3	7.0
Neths.	8	5	4	4	8	7	5.8
Portugal	8	10	7	6	3	11	7.5
Spain	1	10	9	4	5	9	6.3
UK	3	3	1	1	1	1	1.7

Source: based on Grubb and Wells, 1993, apart from * (CEC, 1995d).

The extent to which this national variation can be attributed to policy competition between European countries is difficult to measure. For over a decade, most European countries have experienced strong pressures to deregulate their labour markets, especially in terms of the restrictions on working time, employment protection, and the use of part-time and temporary employment. However, changes in national regulatory environments have usually been prompted by domestic concerns, especially persistently high levels of unemployment across Western Europe and the increasing incidence of part-time and temporary employment. Many governments have increasingly linked labour market rigidities to the rise of long-term unemployment, resulting from a lack of responsiveness of wages, working arrangements and conditions, and ultimately, employment levels to changes in international markets. As unemployment became a key policy priority throughout Western Europe, especially in the wake of the recession of the early 1990s, governments identified aspects of regulation - notably those relating to pay and employment conditions - as contributing to the microeconomic labour market rigidities at the level of individual enterprises. In other words, debate over labour market deregulation has been largely inspired by consideration of the barriers to *existing* firms expanding their employment, not the attraction of external companies as additional employers. Nevertheless, it has not prevented some governments taking advantage of the beneficial impact of deregulation in improving their country's image to foreign investors.

These pressures are seen clearly in the example of Spain. As seen in the table above, Spain has high levels of employment protection, particularly with regard to dismissal, the use of part-time employment, and weekend working and night shifts. Partly as a result of the country's high unemployment and partly because of a strong 'jobs-for-life' industrial tradition, the country retains relatively stringent controls on employee dismissal. Dismissed employees have been able to receive redundancy pay for unfair dismissal at a rate of 45 days per year worked, up to a maximum of 42 months, representing one of the highest rates in Western Europe. The regulations have encouraged the use of temporary employment and been a factor in the country's unemployment, which remains high by Western European standards. Responding to a widely-recognised need to reform the system, successive Spanish governments have attempted to introduce legislative reforms in spite of strong union opposition to extensive changes to the system (*Financial Times*, 1997b).

Nevertheless, evidence suggests that relative labour market standards have been highlighted by some countries in competition for FDI, even if labour market deregulation as a whole is in response to more domestic considerations. In particular, UK governments have claimed that policies of removing labour market rigidities were key in making the country the foremost destination for European and non-European foreign investment throughout the 1980s and 1990s. The UK was notably active in removing several institutional mechanisms for determining pay and reforming industrial relations, with the combined effect of increasing the autonomy of individual plants/enterprises in setting their own pay and employment conditions with local workforces. Although these reforms were largely undertaken without specific reference to foreign investment, they were received well by foreign investors, owing to the importance they place on local bargaining autonomy. The most visible mark of the Conservative government's determination to remain the most deregulated country in Western Europe was the refusal to sign the Social Chapter in the 1991 Maastricht Treaty, as it was feared that the Social Chapter would result in a 'levelling up' of UK standards to the EU level. Subsequent disputes between the Conservative government and the European Commission - most famously over the 48-hour working week decision in the EU - reinforced the underlying differences between the UK and the rest of the Continent.

Although it has never been clearly established that the UK's more flexible labour markets offer incoming investors substantial advantages not available in more restrictive European locations, the widespread perception of UK labour market flexibility has reinforced its inward investment image. The issue of foreign investment was frequently cited by government ministers as a critical reason for resisting calls to join the Social Chapter, and the relative lack of UK employment protection regulations has been a consistent feature of its inward investment promotion campaigns and literature. Numerous anecdotal accounts of the importance of flexible labour markets by new UK investors suggest that the perception was strong among many multinationals as well. In a recent business survey, nearly two-thirds of EU corporate investors regarded the UK as a more desirable location because of the opt-out (*Corporate Location*, 1995). Moreover, a sense of the competitive aspect of the UK's labour market is reflected in the accusations of social dumping made against the UK by other European countries, particularly loudly during the Hoover affair outlined above, but with regularity in the period between the Social Chapter's signing and the new Labour government's announcement that the UK would finally join.

An element of policy competition can also be found in the recent measures by other European countries to deregulate. In Germany, deregulation of labour market gathered pace during the 1980s at both national level (through legislative changes to working conditions) and within sectors (through collective agreements between industry unions and companies). The combined effect of these changes has been to simplify flexible working time arrangements and increase the ease of employers using part-time and temporary workers, often in exchange for concessions on shorter working weeks.

This has partly taken place because of awareness that labour market regulation - and labour costs in general - has been contributing to investment flight from Germany. Although there has been relatively little concern that Germany has not attracted levels of foreign investment commensurate with its economic strength - indeed, as noted in earlier chapters, federal and regional governments have traditionally given FDI promotion less priority than other European countries - anxieties have risen about the surge of outward investment by domestic companies, especially to lower-cost locations in Central and Eastern Europe. Recent surveys show that high labour costs and a lack of labour market flexibility - especially with regard to working time, resulting in difficulties in maximising machine operating time and overall plant utilisation - have prompted over a quarter of German industrial companies to consider shifting production abroad over the next three years (*Financial Times*, 1997c). With unemployment in Germany having risen to unusually high levels, attempts to remove these labour market rigidities can be seen in the federal government's reform of working time legislation and the increasing number of collective agreements between large companies and unions in which more flexible shift systems have been agreed to prevent production relocations out of Germany. Indeed, agreements are increasingly being reached at plant level in spite of the existing regulatory regime.

Perhaps the most striking evidence of policy competition in Western Europe has been the attempts at the EU level to provide regulation of employment protection measures through the Social Chapter. As noted earlier, the Social Chapter was inspired by the perceived need to provide a common 'floor' to social and working standards across the EU and prevent any fraying of 'social cohesion' as a result of the industrial restructuring catalysed by the Single Market programme. Explicit concerns were expressed in the negotiation of the Social Chapter about potential competitive bidding for foreign investment between countries in labour market regulation and resurfaced intermittently as part of the social dumping debate.

Although there has theoretically been a 'social dimension' to the Community from its inception - the Treaty of Rome included broad commitments by the Member States to improve working and living conditions - social measures at the EU level have been increasing in importance in recent years. This new prominence of EU social policy should be seen in the context of other policy developments within the Union. As part of the Single European Act - which legitimised the Single Market programme - special emphasis was given to harmonising health and safety standards out of concern that increasing competition among

European firms should not lead to worsening employment conditions. As extensive deregulation of trade barriers was occurring through the Single Market programme, it was increasingly felt necessary within the Community to prevent deregulation taking place in social and environmental standards.

As a result, a statement of objectives relating to the European social dimension was made with the Social Charter in 1989. The Social Charter formed the basis for the discussions of the social and employment aspects of the Treaty of Union in 1991. New articles in the Treaty included employment and social protection, dialogue between management and labour, the development of human resources and reducing social exclusion. Under the Treaty, the Council was allowed to act by qualified majority voting on health and safety issues, working conditions, sexual equality in the workplace and the integration of the socially-excluded into the labour market. Issues requiring unanimous support included social security, protection of redundant workers, representation of workers' and employers' interests, and financing measures for employment and job creation. Pay and the rights of association and striking were specifically excluded. As a result of the UK Government's opposition to EU action in many of these areas, the other eleven Member States agreed to these issues in a protocol attached to the main body of the Treaty.

The Social Chapter defined the issue of policy competition as a straightforward conflict between the UK and the rest of the EU. As has been seen, while the UK has been at the forefront of labour market deregulation, it has not been the only country to remove labour market rigidities out of concern at rising unemployment and lost investment. Yet the majority of measures put forward (at least initially) through the Social Chapter have tended to emphasise UK differences with the rest of the EU, notably the works council directive and the 48-hour working week initiative.

The impact of the Social Chapter on foreign investment relates mainly to the extent to which its implementation will change differences in national labour market regulations sufficiently to influence the investment decisions of multinational companies. The chief ways in which such differences will be altered are twofold: *removing* existing differences as a result of harmonisation and by *exacerbating* differences between participants and non-participants of the agreement (ie. the UK and the rest of the EU). Since 1991, several social policy measures have been suggested and drafted. To date, few have been introduced and made fully operational through the Social Chapter, and their impact on foreign investment has been limited. Many multinationals based in the UK have complied with the works council directive - whereby large multinationals must establish a workers council to discuss significant company changes - because of their requirement to do so in their Continental operations, reducing the force of the UK's opt-out as a location factor. The working time directive - in which a maximum working week of 48 hours was stipulated - has been imposed on the UK in line with other EU countries because of its adoption as a health and safety measure, outside of the Social Chapter. In any case, this directive has been weakened by the number of sectoral/job category derogations that it allows. More significantly, several key areas likely to affect labour market flexibility - and in consequence, company investment decisions - have not been addressed by EU social policy, especially atypical employment issues (such as whether part-time and temporary workers should be given the same protection rights as 'long-term' workers) and collective bargaining at national and sectoral levels.

The EU's efforts to regulate policy competition in this field stands in sharp contrast to its success with regional incentives. Its jurisdiction has been limited by the non-participation of one of the key 'competitors' - the UK, though this has changed with the new Labour government signing the Social Chapter - and the limited number of policy areas in which action has taken place. Further, unlike the regulation of incentives, EU action in this area can conflict with other EU goals, particularly the priority currently given to employment creation across Europe. The Commission has recognised that some forms of labour market protection could lead to increasing rigidities in European labour markets, making it more difficult to address the problem of unemployment. Hence, in its efforts to support measures that will reduce long-term unemployment, the European Commission - and many of the individual Member State governments - has echoed UK support for increasing labour market flexibility, both at a macroeconomic as well as an individual company level. While providing a floor for social and employment standards does not necessarily contradict this goal, it has limited the Commission's authority and willingness to limit regulatory differences between Member States.

Conclusions

The relationship between labour market regulation and FDI promotion has been gradually emerging in recent years. As companies assign greater important to production systems and working arrangements that enhance their flexibility, they are also giving more consideration to investment locations that will enable plants to adapt their organisation and employment rapidly to technological and commercial changes. The UK has long taken the lead in drawing attention to the link between labour market flexibility and the attraction of FDI, both in the extensive deregulation of UK employment legislation and in the marketing of the country as the most 'flexible' employment environment in Europe. Its refusal to participate in the Social Chapter for so long may not have had more than symbolic importance, but it became a highly visible feature distinguishing the UK as an investment location. That the strategy has been successful can be seen in the number of investors in the UK emphasising how the perception of UK flexible labour markets affected their decisions, though how important this has been a factor has not been fully assessed.

Policy competition in this area was clearly demonstrated by the tensions that have existed between the UK and other Western European countries over employment regulation, most notably in the Social Chapter and Hoover relocation disputes. Whether such competition has been increasing is less readily known. Labour market deregulation and increasing employment flexibility have been pursued by most European governments over the last decade, but this appears to have been principally prompted by the need to invigorate domestic industry in the face of global pressures, rather than through any form of competition among states, especially for FDI projects (though countries have been quick to use deregulation in promoting themselves to foreign investors). If anything, it suggests that competition may be reduced in future, as the differences in European labour markets and regulatory environments diminish.

The impact of such deregulation on foreign investment could also decline as European policy approaches converge (with the UK committing itself to the Social Chapter and Continental governments adapting the UK's pro-flexibility policy approach). In part, this reflects the decreasing scope for social dumping to occur. Although it is debatable how far social dumping actually took place - apart from a few, publicised examples - it is clear that several multinationals have taken advantage of differences in labour market flexibility to increase productivity in their plants, occasionally by tying investment decisions to workforce concessions. Again, it is uncertain what role policy has played in this process, as companies have not been responding directly to labour market regulation, but their workforces' willingness (and ability) to increase flexible working arrangements.

The issue has highlighted the fact that several FDI processes take place outside view and beyond the influence of policy competition. Labour market flexibility appears to be an important factor in restructuring between the different plants of a multinational, not only in shaping negotiations between management and workforce but also in the investment decisions determining the expansion and contraction of individual plants. Such changes in the investment balance between different plants are not easily detected, given the problems in obtaining data. This 'invisible restructuring' may account for a substantial share of investment flows in Europe, perhaps one that will rise as European integration pressures - through the Single Market effects and the enlargement of the EU - encourage multinationals to consider new investment location patterns. Policy approaches to attracting FDI have hitherto focused on influencing greenfield decisions - for example, through financial and fiscal incentive offers - but in future, governments may give greater weight to policies that influence the operating environments for investors, such as labour market regulation.

Moreover, there remain other areas of labour market policy in which governments may be tempted to pursue FDI competition. As noted in the previous chapter, European Commission control of financial incentives could stimulate some governments to investigate alternative policy options for attracting foreign investors. Such policies already include the use of tax, and there is certainly scope for governments to use social security tax rates to influence location decisions. Although governments do not explicitly change social security payment systems to influence internationally-mobile investments as yet, the increasing shift of the tax burden from capital to labour in Western Europe may offer opportunities for governments to pursue competition in policy areas that remain outside EU purview.

9   Conclusions

PHILIP RAINES AND ROSS BROWN

This study set out to address three questions regarding the competition for foreign direct investment between European governments. First, it assessed the extent of policy competition in Europe, particularly how competition has influenced the development of policy approaches to attracting FDI - in terms of the importance given to the objective, the variety of policy instruments used and the resources allocated to it, insofar as this can be measured. Second, the study considered whether such competition had been rising in recent years as well as the factors behind any intensification of inter-governmental rivalry. Lastly, it evaluated the effects of policy competition to determine whether competition has led to a 'positive-sum game' - by which competition has encouraged an overall rise in FDI and resulted in more open national markets and a more secure legal environment - or if competition has led to incentives 'bidding wars' between governments and degradation of labour and environmental standards.

The final chapter of the study summarises the three sets of issues. In addition, it suggests future directions in which policy can enhance the positive effects of competition while reducing the negative impacts.

Is there policy competition in Europe?

The incentive for governments to compete for FDI in Europe has clearly grown. FDI in Western Europe has continued to increase substantially over the last few decades in line with the global growth in foreign investment flows, but it has been given significant regional impetus in recent years by EU deregulation and economic integration measures, most visibly through the Single Market programme. Not only has this attracted considerable investment from outside Western Europe - especially from Japan and the US - but it has encouraged extensive restructuring of investment between European countries. More dramatically, in Central and Eastern Europe, the revolutions from 1989 onwards transformed the FDI profiles of most CEE countries, not just in terms of the volume of flows but more significantly, the importance placed on foreign investment as an agent of economic restructuring. In almost every European country then, FDI has grown as a share of GDP over the past decade.

It is difficult to gauge whether the growth in FDI or increasing governmental interest in attracting FDI came first, as the two processes have taken place simultaneously. Greater sensitivity to the potential gains of FDI to national, regional and local economies has been demonstrated in three trends in recent years: the growth in the number of inward investment agencies, the intensity of their competition and the wave of deregulatory activity that has taken place in Europe. First, agencies specifically established to promote inward investment have proliferated in recent years. New national agencies have been established in countries such as Finland, Sweden and Greece as well as across CEE to undertake foreign investment promotion for the first time. Existing agencies have expanded their networks of representative offices and become autonomous organisations rather than subsumed within government ministries, as in France. Similarly, the attraction and support of inward investment has been highlighted in recent regional development strategies, reflecting the increasing recognition of the value of FDI in local economic development through a series of employment, income, technology transfer and best-practice effects.

Second, in pursuing foreign investment, competition between agencies - especially in Western Europe - appears to have grown steadily in recent years. The change is difficult to quantify, but is evident from the greater publicity given to inter-agency rivalry Individual reports abound of companies being bombarded by inquiries from inward investment agencies when announcing their intention to locate new projects. Anecdotal evidence from investing companies and location consultants suggests that an element of bidding is frequently present where several countries and regions try to win particularly large projects. At national level, there has also been concern that the often-intense rivalry between regional agencies can be counter-productive, resulting in a bidding up of financial incentive packages to the detriment of the country as a whole. Indeed, the UK is currently reviewing its institutional arrangements regarding inward investment attraction in order to prevent excessive competition between different regions (especially Wales and Scotland) for foreign investment projects.

Lastly, national economic environments have become more open to foreign investors across Europe. In Western Europe, deregulation of mergers and acquisitions activity has occurred in nearly all countries - allowing foreign investors to enter into sectors that had previously been restricted or closed - at the same time as an increasing number of countries have been displaying more favourable attitudes to foreign investors in terms of liberalised administrative procedures for approving investments and capital controls. Privatisation has created opportunities for foreign investors across the continent, though particularly in CEE, where the restructuring of national industries has been linked to the need to attract foreign companies. This has also intensified the international competition for inward investment - eg. recently, the West Midland in the UK has lost a number of projects to Poland (*Financial Times*,1997a).

In this context, it is worth highlighting the role of the UK in setting much of the competitive agenda. Although the UK was not alone in its early policy support for FDI (eg. Ireland also has a long tradition of attracting foreign investment), the country's remarkable success in consistently capturing the largest share of European and non-European investment - as well as the major role that foreign investment has within regional economies in the UK such as Scotland and Wales - has drawn attention to both its overall attitude and specific policies. Much of the recent competition for foreign investment can be attributed in large part to the UK's emphasis on combining a well-organised institutional structure for attracting FDI with policies to create a favourable environment for foreign investors.

Nevertheless, to date, policy competition in Europe has existed within firm limits. For the region as a whole, competition has been cast principally in terms of the internal rivalry within Europe for mobile investment projects, in which national (and increasingly, sub-national) authorities view each other as their main competitors. Competition with other parts of the world has been limited - indeed, few inward investment agencies regard non-European countries on their borders, such as Mediterranean Africa, as significant rivals. Although locations further afield (in Asia and the US) often compete for investments made by large multi-plant companies, governments primarily view other European locations as their main investment rivals. For example, with regards to competition in financial incentives, grant offers are made on the basis of what agencies elsewhere in Europe may be expected to offer, and rarely on the anticipated incentives available from non-European locations.

In CEE, concerted competition is limited currently by lack of government resources for the attraction of FDI and lack of experience in most countries. Although the importance of foreign investment to industrial restructuring continues to be enshrined in macroeconomic policy, this has largely taken the form of creating opportunities for foreign companies to participate in existing CEE ventures by creating a stable legal and economic environment for investors. In addition, CEE governments and local authorities act in an *ad hoc* manner by offering incentives to major FDI projects, creating special economic zones and greenfield site preparation. CEE governments have only started to engage in widespread competition for mobile investments, commonly through special tax concessions (a policy instrument used more frequently in CEE than in Western Europe). However, it is debatable how much influence government policy can affect investment decisions, given the overwhelming importance of location factors beyond direct policy control, such as labour costs and market proximity.

In Western Europe, the limits of policy competition can be seen in the use of the key policy instrument for attracting foreign investment: financial grants. Although nearly all Western European governments operate an incentive scheme for attracting large, mobile investments (though rarely explicitly so), there is little evidence to suggest that competition for FDI projects has been accelerating rapidly. Trends in regional incentive expenditure, award rates and eligible locations do not support the thesis that competition for projects has altered the scale or design of governments' main policy instruments for attracting FDI.

It is worth emphasising that expenditure on incentive schemes has declined or remained relatively constant in most countries, and overall, the cost of FDI policy has accounted for small shares of government expenditure. Relative to other industrial policy areas, the attraction of FDI has not been a policy priority in Western Europe. According to Table 4.6 above, between 1989 and 1993, only one country spent more than half a percent of GDP on the main incentive schemes for attracting foreign investment (Ireland), as compared with government expenditure on the main R&D industrial measures and projects, in which only Greece, Ireland, Portugal and Spain have an annual average which is *less* than half a percent of GDP (OECD, 1996c).

The limits on competition reveal the importance of inter-governmental regulation, especially at the Community level. The system for monitoring and curbing state subsidies in the EU is unique. Through its controls of State aids, the European Commission has been active - with the authority of the founding Treaties of the Community - in restricting the extent to which competition for mobile investment projects has led to competitive outbidding. In particular, support for large projects has been confined to specially-designated areas (ie. problem regions). Nevertheless, the system of subsidy discipline does have weaknesses: Commission limits on award rates have been criticised for their lack of 'bite'; the controls tend not to extend beyond national financial incentives and do not easily capture regional/local measures, especially where they are of a non-financial nature (such as training support and site preparation); and the Commission remains susceptible to political pressure from the Member States, especially with respect to 'exceptional' cases of government aid. Nevertheless, the Commission's control of incentives has been broadly effective in that it has resulted in a robust regulatory framework, recognised by Member States and backed by judicial review. Further, it has shown itself adaptable to extension across the continent, as seen in the application of Community guidelines to the countries of the European Economic Area and CEE countries linked to the EU through the Europe Agreements.

Is competition for FDI increasing between European governments?

The levels of investment in Europe are likely to remain high in the near future. Further economic integration in Europe - through European Monetary Union and enlargement of the EU - should encourage new investment from outside as well as within Europe. The parallel processes of industrial restructuring in Western Europe (as a result of the Single Market programme *inter alia*) and CEE (through further economic liberalisation, market stability and growth, and remaining privatisation measures) will generate new investment opportunities in the region over the coming decade.

In Western Europe, much of this investment is anticipated to take the form of re-investments rather than greenfields, though increasing investment from new source countries such as South Korea point to a continuing stream of greenfield projects for which countries will compete. As a result, the challenges for policy will shift in emphasis, away from an exclusive focus on attracting new projects towards a concern with expanding and upgrading existing investments. In this context, competition from CEE is likely to become a more important factor than it has been hitherto, putting pressure on governments to find ways of *retaining* investment (an issue of primary concern to some countries already, notably Germany). This may lead to a diminished interest in incentive-based approaches and the development of more innovative FDI policies, particularly those which concentrate on maximising the value of a FDI project's contribution to the local economy rather than simply the number of projects won (eg. by encouraging the location of higher value-added activities, such as R&D).

In CEE, as individual economies stabilise and grow (albeit at differing rates), the region should experience an increase in FDI flows, especially from non-European investing countries which have been cautious to enter until recently (of which, Japan is the most prominent). At the same time, the number of rival locations for FDI projects in CEE should rise as more countries follow the economic trajectories of the leading Visegrad economies. In response, CEE countries can be expected to use financial and fiscal incentives more competitively to distinguish their locations, though as in Western Europe, great importance will continue to be placed on policies affecting other location factors (particularly with respect to the quality of local infrastructure and workforce skills).

Community controls on incentive-based competition will keep rivalry within prescribed limits across Europe, as prospective Community members (including CEE countries) are required to adopt Commission State aids guidelines. A key effect of this regulation is likely to be the pressure put on governments to explore other policy options for promoting and retaining FDI. One area where this has already been visible is the use of tax by governments. A distinction needs to made here between explicit tax *incentives*, as operated within designated areas along similar lines to financial incentives, and the wider use of tax *systems* to encourage foreign investment. In general, most Western European countries do not have tax concessions targeted at the attraction of FDI (as is the case in CEE), though many governments advertise their low rate of corporate tax in FDI promotion (such as the UK and Sweden). However, in some countries, tax appears to be a crucial instrument of FDI policy, especially in Belgium, Ireland and the Netherlands. Such usage lies outside Commission regulatory control, as tax operation cannot easily be classified under State aid guidelines. To date, this has not yet resulted in an accelerating growth in the number of FDI tax concession schemes (at least in Western Europe), but concern with rising policy competition in this area can be seen in the desire among many Member States to establish a Community code on tax breaks for mobile investment.

In non-financial policy areas, it is likely that policy competition will remain present, though perhaps muted. With regards to labour market policies, competition continues to be a significant factor in policy-making. The UK has long highlighted its liberal employment laws as a location factor, prompting accusations by other European governments of inciting competitive deregulation. Fear of competition in this area has resulted in some, albeit minor, regulation at Community level through the Social Chapter and a moderate movement towards more deregulated labour markets in other European countries. Moreover, scope exists for competition in other aspects of labour market policy, most notably in social security tax systems, as multinationals may be increasingly sensitive to non-wage cost differentials in influencing location decisions.

Environmental regulation will also continue to have a notable - though restrained - impact on FDI patterns. As with labour market regulation, the Community is playing a greater role in setting common regulatory floors, though unlike labour market standards, there has been little substance to the fears that foreign investors are trying to subvert national regulation by taking advantage of lower standards. Increasingly, *higher* environmental standards have been highlighted as a location factor in attracting FDI. Although governments are less likely to pursue competitive deregulation of standards than hitherto, Western European governments have adopted more strategic approaches in their application of environmental standards.

The use of a wider range of policies to attract FDI raises important questions about the regulation of competition. On the one hand, the jurisdiction of the European Commission is constrained by the competencies assigned to it under the Treaties. Hence, the ability to regulate the use of tax is limited because the Commission is not authorised to supervise direct taxation systems, only those features of the tax system that constitute State aid. Similarly, the attempt to develop EU-wide approaches to social and employment legislation was hindered by the UK's refusal to sign the Social Chapter.

Regulation has also become more difficult as competition develops in areas where it is difficult to identify how the Commission can usefully be active. Definitional issues are central here. At what point can a tax system's design be regarded as providing an unfair competitive advantage to a country in attracting foreign investment? Is it possible to separate labour market legislation aimed at foreign investors by lowering employment protection standards (and hence be interpreted as 'social dumping') from measures intended to reduce unemployment by increasing national labour market flexibility? The uncertainty allows considerable scope for future policy competition, though to date, these options have been relatively unexplored by competing governments.

Yet in setting the limits for regulation, policy competition has also revealed the strength of the existing framework. In establishing the principle of a 'level playing field' for FDI competition within the EU, Member State governments have been sensitive to incentive and regulatory 'bidding wars', even suggesting the development of Commission controls over new policy instruments, such as tax. While Community regulation is only effective with the broad political support of the Member States, by the same token, the existence of the regulatory framework may have concentrated Member State attention on the dangers of unrestrained competition, even in policy areas outside of Commission competence. Moreover, as more European countries aim to associate with or join the EU, Community rules will act as a limiting force over a wider area of the region in future.

What have been the effects of policy competition?

It is perhaps surprising that the increasing competition for FDI in Europe has not been matched by greater understanding of the overall benefits of investment or the impacts of specific policies. Much is known about how foreign investors can affect a local economy. The benefits of FDI projects can include direct employment and income gains, and a series of less tangible impacts, such as multiplier effects through local suppliers and services, the transfer of new technologies, production systems and management practices. Foreign investment can also result in the elimination of local competition, poaching of key workers from other companies and a risk of branch-plant dependency. While government policies have been generally careful to favour FDI projects that are likely to produce the former set of effects (insofar as possible), few quantification exercises have been undertaken by governments. Methodological problems - especially the difficulty of determining the counterfactual (ie. what would have happened in the absence of government policy) - ensure that cost-benefit analyses of specific policies will always be hedged with considerable uncertainty.

As a result, the evidence in determining the costs and benefits of foreign investment has been mixed. For example, in the UK, numerous government-commissioned evaluations have concluded that on balance, the effects have been largely positive (see, for example, PACEC, 1995). By contrast, studies in Ireland have shown that the contributions of foreign companies to Irish GDP, export and employment growth have been greatly exaggerated and that the costs of disinvestment have not been taken into account fully (Shirlow, 1995). For CEE countries, it is even more difficult to make assessments at this point, as the principal objective of attracting foreign investors - to stimulate industrial restructuring that would improve overall economic competitiveness - is a process that will remain underway for some time to come (so the anticipated benefits of FDI have yet to materialise fully).

Given this continuing debate, it is difficult to assess properly the effects of policy competition. For incentive-based policies, the problems are particularly acute. Business surveys have repeatedly found that financial incentives have limited significance as a location factor, and yet it is clear from the individual accounts of competition for large projects, that substantial awards can have a major role in winning investments, if only by neutralising the impact of rivals' incentive offers. The secrecy surrounding incentive offers and company decision-making renders it almost impossible to conclude on how much incentive offers influence location decisions. Moreover, it is by no means clear that regional incentive policies are able to achieve their primary objective - to stimulate economic activity in less-developed regions - when considered at a European level. The substantial regional variation in incentive expenditure and the absence of a correlation between incentive spending and GDP per capita suggest that policy competition continues to favour the more prosperous countries.

For similar reasons, the role of tax policy in attracting FDI cannot easily be measured. Information on the impact of tax systems on FDI location decisions is as scarce and unreliable as for financial incentives. The problems are compounded in the case of taxation due to the extra complications in calculating the policy cost of a tax system designed to entice foreign investors (in terms of foregone revenue).

Nevertheless, with regards to regulatory policies, it can be argued that policy competition has had distinctively beneficial effects. Although it is not clear whether some companies have been taking advantage of differences in employment and environmental standards at the expense of their workforces, regulatory differences have not resulted in a competitive degradation of standards between governments. Indeed, in the case of environmental standards, the opposite appears to be the case - policy competition has *raised* standards across much of Europe. With respect to fear of social dumping, while its influence on policy competition is diminishing, too little is understood of the impact of labour market standards on investment patterns to determine whether policy-makers in the future may see this as an area of active FDI promotion (especially in the area of competition in social security tax rates, as noted above).

Moreover, where competitive deregulation has taken place, it seems to have resulted in a larger number of economies becoming more open to international trade and investment. If anything, liberalisation of sectors to foreign acquisitions, demonopolisation and privatisation trends, and relaxation of capital controls have tended to reduce policy competition between governments. It has diminished the relevance of government attitudes to investors as a location factor in Europe as well as contributed to a more even distribution of FDI in the continent.

This raises the wider issue of the effect of policy competition on the policy-making process as a whole. Although governments tend not to develop all-embracing 'FDI policies' as such, they have developed institutional bridges between different policy areas in their efforts to attract investment. Different policies have been brought together in different ways: superficially in terms of the general marketing undertaken by inward investment agencies (eg. when promoting the advantages of operating in a particular location), but more substantially, when IIAs put together financial and fiscal incentives for specific projects and 'smooth' the way where investors face a series of potential regulatory hurdles, particularly in CEE. In policy-making itself, FDI has also established itself as a visible determinant on the design of policy, not necessarily as the primary factor, but increasingly as an issue which cannot be ignored when policy directly affects the ability of countries and regions to compete for projects.

How can policy enhance the positive effects of FDI competition in future?

As has been seen, substantial uncertainty remains in assessing the effects of policy competition in Europe. In spite of these difficulties, it is still possible to identify areas where the design and delivery of existing policies could be improved in order to increase the positive and limit the negative effects of policy competition. In general, these are policies which raise the contribution of FDI projects to local economies, enhance the industrial competitiveness of local economies in order to attract inward investment, remove regulatory discrimination between domestic and foreign companies (allowing greater competition), and reinforce the regulatory framework restricting policy competition between countries. These policies options are outlined under the following headings: inward investment promotion; the use of financial and fiscal incentives; non-incentive policies; and the different circumstances affecting policy in CEE.

Inward Investment Promotion

FDI promotion will become more sophisticated as rivalry between governments remains strong. In order to avoid excessive competition for FDI between countries, inward investment agencies should adopt specific strategies in foreign investment promotion. In particular, IIAs could benefit from a more systematic approach towards attracting FDI which takes into account the economic impact of projects and the location's competitive advantage. This would involve a careful assessment of the needs of the local economy in terms of the *type* of projects, companies and sectors that are desirable to target as well as can be feasibly won. For example, agencies may concentrate on what parts of the value chain are weak within an emerging local industrial cluster. As such, agencies may be less likely to compete for any significant mobile projects, only those fitting more detailed specifications.

Further, IIAs could begin to focus more on upgrading the overall quality of FDI through better-developed aftercare services, often the most neglected aspect of FDI strategy. Policy would shift away from the exclusive attraction of greenfield investments towards increasing the level and value of links between existing investors and the local economy, principally through winning expansion investments. Although (as argued in Chapter 3) greenfield site investment brings enormous potential benefits to CEE and is likely to form a major plank in their FDI attraction measures, there are some tentative signs that IIAs in Europe generally are beginning to move in this direction. For example, the Invest in Sweden Agency are currently devising an after-care policy which seeks to maximise re-investments made by existing foreign-owned companies in Sweden.

This kind of identification and targeting may be better achieved at local rather than national level in many countries, where the FDI requirements of an economy can be more clearly articulated. However, where FDI promotion can be decentralised effectively (at present, more likely in Western rather than Eastern Europe), it will still be necessary to retain national controls on the activities of sub-national agencies, in order to limit competitive outbidding within countries (as recent spats between Scottish and national inward investment authorities in the UK have demonstrated). Moreover, such controls should be extended to govern the measures used by local authorities as well as agencies within the national structure of FDI promotion. This might be most efficiently undertaken by devolving promotional activities - including regional marketing and FDI identification and targeting - to a regional (and where appropriate, sub-regional) level, but maintaining strict national guidelines on the use of financial incentives and other concessions.

Financial and Fiscal Incentives

Incentives have often been criticised for their failure to encourage inward investors to increase the value of their projects to a local economy over time. Hence, in the use of financial incentives, there may be a strong argument for their 'calibration' so that the highest awards levels go to FDI projects which have the most significant long-term spin-off effects for the local economy.

At present, most investment projects are valued in terms of their direct employment and income effects. Financial incentives place little emphasis on other benefits from projects, notably technology transfer and skills effects. While this may be appropriate for highly-underdeveloped economies (where low income levels and high unemployment are acute), it could be argued that some regions and countries should increasingly focus on improving the quality of their investments. The positive effects of policy competition would then be enhanced as governments sought to attract higher-quality investments, perhaps by stipulating a timetable for upgrading particular investments, the presence of value-added activities and moderate local content requirements in incentive awards. Policy-makers could make this approach more appealing to foreign investors through government commitments to invest in the local supplier infrastructure and workforce skills. The aim would be to increase long-term cooperation between foreign investors and governments, leading to a mutually beneficial interdependency.

Given that regional financial incentives are the main policy instrument with which countries use to attract FDI, increasing supranational regulatory control over these incentives would also seem desirable. However, it is questionable to what extent the Commission has already influenced the 'blind auction' process that characterises negotiations between mobile investors and potential host countries. Certainly, competition for inward investment among European countries remains fierce and most governments are secretive about the levels of aid used to attract such projects. An important factor in determining levels of grant offered to mobile projects is the value of offers thought to have been made elsewhere in Western Europe; the growing emphasis on obtaining value for money from regional policy is a far more limiting factor than the Commission's award ceilings. In short, Commission control of regional aids has been distinctly 'one-dimensional', focusing on restricting *where* incentives can be offered, but having little influence on *how much* they are worth.

The relative absence of control over award values has caused concern in a number of quarters. Several options for exercising control over award values are available, including: controlling *expenditure* on regional aids by capping regional aid budgets; controlling awards to highly *capital-intensive* projects, where competition between governments is perhaps fiercest; and controlling *large* individual awards, so that countries with large incentive budgets cannot outbid lesser-resourced countries. The first of these has never been seriously considered by the Commission; the second has been the subject of highly contentious proposals that were subsequently dropped; and the third has resulted in proposals which are likely to be introduced in 1998.

Similar concerns have been expressed about the role of tax in influencing location decisions, but as has already been discussed, regulation has been beset by substantial problems. No ready solutions to the definitional difficulties - ie. what constitutes a tax 'incentive' and when can it be deemed 'unfair' - but the initial international steps to introduce a code controlling the use of tax are encouraging. If nothing else, it suggests that there is a widespread awareness of the dangers of unregulated policy competition in this policy area, and arguably, it is the willingness of individual governments (EU in the first instance, though any agreement is likely to extend to other European governments over time) to cooperate on regulation that is most significant, rather than the short-term details of the cooperation.

Non-Incentive Measures

Although not treated in depth here, in addition to financial measures, there are indications that governments are increasingly using non-incentive policies to improve location attractiveness. As the importance of an investment's operating environment - whether physical infrastructure or more widely-defined as the local business environment - has been consistently highlighted by foreign investors in surveys, governments in Western Europe are giving greater emphasis to policies which can influence both 'hard' factors like physical infrastructure as well as 'soft' ones such as amenity and information networks (Bachtler *et al*, 1996). The ability to alter local economic infrastructure touches on a range of policy areas - particularly regional development, transport and energy - operated at both national and regional levels. While these policies are not necessarily influenced by considerations of FDI attraction, the policies could reinforce the close links between the quality of local infrastructure and locational attractiveness. In order to improve the benefits deriving from FDI - especially with regards to technology and skills transfers - and to encourage the upgrading of existing investments, policy needs to focus on the environmental and infrastructural characteristics of a region that appeal to investors, an issue of particular importance to CEE. Not only does it involve improving the general business environment but also local companies within that environment, notably those that may act as potential suppliers to future and existing investors.

Instead of undifferentiated global investment incentives (for attracting foreign investment as well as supporting the development of local companies), more sophisticated and strategic measures are required to maintain and intensify regional competitiveness and can be conducive to the emergence of a 'creative milieu'. Key features would include amenities (encompassing high-quality health and education services), physical and telecommunications infrastructure, education and training to improve regional strengths in entrepreneurship, management and innovation, and an information and contact-rich environment, especially innovation networks. The type of measures that are typically operated in this context consist of measures relating to: physical infrastructure; training and education support; and research and technology.

- *Physical infrastructure* Infrastructure support is the traditional means used by policy-makers to promote the business environment, especially in problem regions. One approach, already common among northern West European countries, is to provide support for 'local economic infrastructure' including basic utilities, transport facilities and buildings and enterprise centres (often linked to specific investment projects where site development and preparation is undertaken by local authorities). Additional categories of assistance include tourism facilities (as in Germany and Norway) and education and healthcare facilities (as in Switzerland). To date, this type of assistance has been relatively small-scale and secondary to expenditure on financial incentives. A second approach is to address strategic rather than local infrastructure deficits, more common in the least-developed countries, where infrastructure assistance (including road/rail links and telecoms) dominates regional policy plans and budgets and outweighs spending on financial incentives. For example, telecommunication developments to promote home-working and the location of the back-office, administrative functions of large companies have been pursued in peripheral regions, such as the ISDN network constructed in the Highlands and Islands region of the UK.

- *Training and education*   A commitment to human resource development is widely promoted as an important part of regional development strategies, and as a corollary, the attraction of FDI. Unlike in parts of Asia where policies towards FDI are heavily geared towards up-skilling, regional policy in Western Europe has only limited exposure in this area (Brown, 1996). Training qualifies for support under certain investment incentives, and enterprise training services are also provided in a number of countries. Individual-oriented employment services operate in some countries to support the unemployed - as, for example, in Austria - and policy coordination is attempted in other countries to try to promote the labour element of regional policy. One area where policy has been proactive is the development of measures to improve potential suppliers for foreign investors through training, installing quality standards and assisting with the adoption of just-in-time production systems, particularly by regional development agencies in Scotland and Wales.

- *Research and technology*   The final group of business environment measures addresses research and technology development, particularly in problem regions, which are widely recognised to suffer various constraints which hamper technological change. Policy-makers have experienced some difficulties in gaining leverage to this area which can be very costly and, as with labour market issues, tends to be dominated by sectoral considerations. This is a worrying omission given the potential role foreign-owned firms can play in technological development. Policies designed to encourage R&D networking between investors, local firms and research institutions could potentially deepen the investment presence and value in local economies. At present only a limited degree of financial assistance is incorporated in a number of regional assistance packages, such as the costs of technical studies, the acquisition of technology, patents and licenses, the development of prototypes and the application of new technology. Some countries - like Austria, the UK and Norway - also operate specific innovation schemes in problem regions, but, as in the UK, often these exclude large firms.

CEE Policy

Finally, it is important to consider the future directions of FDI policy in CEE, particularly given the importance that inward investment has in the continuing process of economic restructuring. As concluded in Chapter 3, in future, CEE governments are likely to compete more fiercely with each other for FDI, but ironically, this will be occurring at a time when they may find the policy options available to them limited by the external pressures under which they are operating. Policy decisions will be determined by their continuing need for inward investment in the absence of domestic capital sources, intensifying competition with other CEE governments, limited budgetary resources for FDI promotion and the Community's regulatory controls on industrial policy (as imposed through the Association Agreements). Future policy will continue to emphasise the attraction of inward investment as a priority objective and the attention is likely to remain on the volume of foreign investment rather than its quality (unlike the situation in Western Europe). As a result, there may be less scope for considering a range of policy 'cocktails' than in Western Europe.

In any case, it is likely that policy's impact on the location factors for CEE investment may remain minor compared to the continuing role of labour costs and market proximity, though this is unlikely to diminish competition between the different countries and regions. Some internal policy measures will have a significant impact on location decisions - notably measures to improve local physical and business infrastructure - but from the perspective of most CEE governments, the main policy step that can be taken to ensure the continuing flow of inward investment is external: membership of the EU.

Where CEE governments can act effectively is in developing the administrative structures for pursuing FDI policy, especially with regards to the clear division of responsibilities between local and national agencies, the importance of establishing links between both levels, the professionalism and experience of FDI promotion officials, clarity in defining the goals of FDI policy and the ability of national policy-makers to bring together different policy areas into a single, comprehensive and coherent policy towards FDI (perhaps a greater priority in CEE than in Western Europe, because of the national importance of FDI in these countries). Clearly, CEE governments can learn much from Western European models of FDI promotion, though care will have to be taken in how to adapt them to their differing circumstances.

Bibliography

Adnett, N. (1996) *European Labour Markets: Analysis and Policy*, Longman, London.

Allen, K., Hull, C. and Yuill, D. (1979) 'Options in Regional Incentive Policy' in Allen, K (ed.) *Balanced National Growth*, Lexington Books, Massachusetts.

Amin, A. and Tomaney, J. (1995) 'The Regional Development Potential of Inward Investment in the Less Favoured Regions of the European Community' in Amin, A. and Tomaney, J. (eds.) *Behind the Myth of European Union*, Routledge, London.

Ashford, N. (1993) 'Understanding Technological Responses of Industrial Firms to Environmental Problems: Implications for Government Policy', in Fischer, K. and Schot, J. (eds.) *Environmental Strategies for Industry: International Perspectives on Research Needs and Policy Implications*, Island Press, Washington DC.

Bachtler, J. and Clement, K. (1990a) *The Impact of the Single European Market on Foreign Direct Investment in the United Kingdom*, HMSO, London.

Bachtler, J. and Clement, K. (1990b) *1992 and Foreign Direct Investment from the United States: The Implications for the United Kingdom*, report for the UK Department of Trade and Industry, London.

Bachtler, J. *et al* (1996) *Regional Policies in EFTA and the EU: A Comparative Assessment*, report for a consortium of EFTA governments, European Policies Research Centre, University of Strathclyde, Glasgow.

Bailey, D., Harte, G. and Sugden, R. (1991) 'Dirigisme at the Core of the French Approach to Inward Investment', *Multinational Business*, vol. 2, pp. 34-43.

Barrel, R. and Pain, N. (1996) 'An Econometric Analysis of US Foreign Direct Investment', *Review of Economics and Statistics*, vol. 78, pp. 200-207.

Barrel, R. and Pain, N. (1997) 'The Growth of Foreign Direct Investment in Europe', *National Institute Economic Review*, vol. 160, pp. 63-75.

Barrett, B., Campbell, R. and Spohn, E. (1993) 'Environment, Development and Inward Investment in the Commonwealth of Independent States', *European Environment*, vol. 5, pp. 2-6.

Begg, H. and McDowell, S. (1986) 'The Effect of Regional Investment Decisions on Company Decisions', *Regional Studies*, vol. 21, pp. 459-70.

Blomstrom, M. and Kokko, A. (1995) *Foreign Direct Investment and Politics: The Swedish Model*, Discussion Paper, no. 1266, Centre for Economic Policy Research, London.

Blomstrom, M. and Kokko, A. (1997) 'How Foreign Investment Affects Host Countries', *Policy Research Working Paper*, no. 1745, International Economics Department, World Bank, Washington DC.

Boss Export-Import (1996) no. 24.

Brown, R. (1996) *Foreign Direct Investment and Regional Economic Development: Backward Electronics Linkages in Scotland and Singapore*, Unpublished Ph.D thesis, University of Strathclyde, Glasgow.

Brown, R., Raines, P. and Bachtler, J. (1997) *Electronics Foreign Direct Investment in Scotland: Lessons for Nordrhein-Westfalen*, Interim report to the Ministerium für Wirtschaft und Mittelstand, Technologie und Verkehr des Landes Nordrhein-Westfalen, unpublished.

Bundesbank (1997) *Deutsche Bundesbank Monthly Report*, August.

Business Central Europe (1995) 'Foreign Investment in Central Europe', May.

CBI (1994) *Controlling State Aids: Making the Single Market Work*, Confederation of British Industry, London.

CCET (1994) *Assessing Investment Opportunities in Economies in Transition*, Centre for Co-operation with Economies in Transition, OECD, Paris.

CEC (1975) *Fifth Report on Competition Policy*, Office for Official Publications of the European Communities, Luxembourg.

CEC (1979) *Communication on Regional Aid Systems*, Official Journal of the European Communities, No. C 31, 3.2.79.

CEC (1988) *Communication on the Method for the Application of Article 92(3)(a) and (c) to Regional Aids,* Official Journal of the European Communities, C 212, 12.8.88.

CEC (1989) *Community Framework on State Aid to the Motor Vehicle Industry,* Official Journal of the European Communities, C 123, 18.5.1989, as amended.

CEC (1990) *Industrial Policy in an Open and Competitive Environment: Guidelines for a Community Approach,* COM(90)556, 16 November, Commission of the European Communities, Brussels.

CEC (1992a) *Code on Aid to the Synthetic Fibres Industry,* Official Journal of the European Communities, C 346, 30.12.92.

CEC (1992b) *Third Survey on State Aids in the European Community in the Manufacturing and Certain Other Sectors,* Commission of the European Communities, Brussels.

CEC (1992c) *Report of the Committee of Independent Experts on Company Taxation,* Office for Official Publications of the European Communities, Luxembourg.

CEC (1993) *New Location Factors for Mobile Investment in Europe,* Regional Development Studies, 6, Commission of the European Communities, Brussels.

CEC (1994a) *Growth, Competitiveness and Employment: The Challenges and Ways Forward into the 21ˢᵗ Century,* White Paper, Commission of the European Communities, Brussels.

CEC (1994b) *XXIIIrd Report on Competition Policy 1993,* Office for Official Publications of the European Communities, Luxembourg.

CEC (1995a) *A Level Playing Field for Direct Investment World-wide,* COM (95) 42, Commission of the European Communities, Brussels.

CEC (1995b) *Fourth Survey on State Aids in the European Community in the Manufacturing and Certain Other Sectors,* COM(95) 365 final, Commission of the European Communities, Brussels.

CEC (1995c) *Competition Law in the European Communities, Volume IIA: Rules Applicable to State Aids,* Office for Official Publications of the European Communities, Luxembourg.

CEC (1995d) 'Performance of the European Union Labour Market', *European Economy, Reports and Studies,* no. 3, Commission of the European Communities, Brussels.

CEC (1996a) *Taxation in the European Union: Report on the Development of Tax Systems*, COM(96) 546 final, Commission of the European Communities, Brussels.

CEC (1996b) *Tax Competition in the European Union*, Note for the Economic and Policy Committee and the Monetary Committee, DGII, Commission of the European Communities, Brussels.

CEC (1997a) *The Phare Programme: An interim evaluation*, Commission of the European Communities, Brussels.

CEC (1997b) *Fifth Survey on State Aids in the European Community in the Manufacturing and Certain Other Sectors*, COM(97) 170 final, Commission of the European Communities, Brussels.

CEC (1997c) *Agenda 2000: for a Stronger and Wider Europe*, COM(97) 2000, Commission of the European Communities, Brussels.

CEC (1997d) *Taxation: Commission Identifies a Series of Measures to Curb Harmful Tax Competition*, IP/97/830, Rapid Database, Commission of the European Communities, Brussels.

CEC (various years) *Survey on State Aids in the European Community in the Manufacturing and Certain Other Sectors,* Commission of the European Communities, Brussels.

Cecchini, P. (1988) *The European Challenge 1992: The Benefits of a Single European Market,* Wildwood House, Aldershot.

Chennells, L. and Griffith, R. (1997) *Taxing Profits in a Changing World*, Institute for Fiscal Studies, London.

Chicoye, C. (1992) 'Regional Impact of the Single European Market in France', *Regional Studies,* vol. 26, pp. 407-11.

Christodoulou, P. (1996) *Inward Investment: An overview and guide to the literature*, The British Library, London.

Clement, K. (1993) 'Promoting Sustainable Development: Environmental Incentives in Denmark and the Netherlands', *European Environment*, vol. 3, pp. 9-13.

Clement, K. (1994a) 'The Role of the Environment and Quality of Life in Business Location Decisions', in Lindström, B. and Frovin, A. (eds.) *Regional Policies and the Environment*, Nordrefo, Stockholm.

Clement, K. (1994b) 'Government, Industry and Environment: A Review of Policy Initiatives designed to promote Sustainable Development' in Owiklinski, H. and Owsinski, J. (eds.) *Nordic-Baltic Europe is*

Restructuring: Looking for the Integration Fits, Interfaces Institute, Warsaw.

Clement, K. (1997) 'Investing in Europe: Government Support for Environmental Technology', in Ledgerwood, G. (ed.) *Greening the Boardroom: Corporate Governance and Business Sustainability*, Greenleaf Publishing, Sheffield.

Clement, K. and Bachtler, J. (1997) 'Regional Development and Environmental Gain: Strategic Assessment in the Structural Funds', *European Environment*, vol. 7, pp. 7-15.

Cominotti, R. and Mariotti, S. (1994) *Italia Multinazionale 1994*, Etas Libri.

Corporate Location (1995) 'Annual Investment Intentions Survey', September/October.

Corporate Location (1996a) 'Sweden Top for US Investors', September/October.

Corporate Location (1996b) 'A User's Guide: Inward Investment Agencies', November/December.

Corporate Location (1996c) 'From $100 million to $3.4 billion', May-June.

Corporate Location (1996d) 'Hyundai's Hunt for Chip Skills', November/December.

Corporate Location (1997) 'The Control Centre for Eastern Europe', March/April.

CSO (various years) *Report: Census of Production*, HMSO, London.

Cushman, D. (1985) 'Real Exchange Rate Risk, Expectations, and the Level of Direct Investment', *Review of Economics and Statistics*, 67, pp. 297-308.

Deloitte and Touche and Stanford University Graduate School of Business Public Management Programme (1990) *The Environmental Transformation of US Industry: A Survey of US Industrial Corporations Environmental Strategies, Management Policies and Perceptions*, Stanford University Press, Stanford.

Dicken, P. (1994) 'Global-Local Tensions: Firms and States in the Global Space-Economy', *Economic Geography*, vol. 70, pp. 101-128.

Döhrn, R. (1996) 'Direktinvestitionen und Sachkapitalbildung - Statistische Unterschiede und ihre ökonomischen Implikationen,' *RWI-Mitteilungen*, no. 47, pp. 19-34.

Dunning, J. (1993) *Multinational Enterprises and the Global Economy*, Addison-Wesley, Wokingham.

Dunning, J. (1997) 'The European Internal Market Programme and Inbound Foreign Direct Investment', *Journal of Common Market Studies*, vol. 35, pp. 1-30.

The Economist (1989) 'Set up or Stay out', 18 February.

The Economist (1992) 'Aid Addicts', 8 August.

The Economist (1993) 'Green Account', 4 September.

The Economist (1994) 'Banned Aid', 19 November.

The Economist (1996a) 'Bribing for Britain', 8 June.

The Economist (1996b) 'Europe's Back Office', 16 November.

EIRR (1993) 'The Hoover Affair and Social Dumping', *European Industrial Relations Review*, no. 230, pp. 14-20.

EIRR (1994) 'Industrial Relations and Industrial Location - A Case Study of Mercedes-Benz', *European Industrial Relations Review*, no. 244, 12-15.

EIU (1995) *Country Reports: Hungary,* Economist Intelligence Unit, London.

Ernst and Young (1995) *Regions of the New Europe*, Ernst & Young, London.

Estrin, S. and Richet, X. (1996) *A Comparison of Foreign Direct Investments in Bulgaria, The Czech Republic and Slovenia*, ACE Project Report, Z/9109/94/0622-R.

European Voice (1997a) 'No End to Tax-Break Beauty Contest', 20-26 November.

European Voice (1997b) 'Member States Agree to Curb 'Predatory' Tax Breaks', 26 June-2 July.

Eurostat (1995) *European Union Direct Investment 1984-93*, Office for Official Publications of the European Commission, Luxembourg.

Ferner, A. (1994) 'Multinational Companies and Human Resource Management: An Overview of Research Issues', *Human Resource Management Journal*, vol. 4, pp. 79-102.

Financial Times (1995) 'Hunt for Cheap Workers', 24 October.

Financial Times (1996a) 'German Make Play for More Investment', 28 June.

Financial Times (1996b) 'The Aidbusters Charter', 14 November.

Financial Times (1996c) 'Inward Investment into the UK', special section, 18 July.

Financial Times (1997a) 'Losing out to Competitors in the East', 20 November.

Financial Times (1997b) 'A Step in the Right Direction', 27 May.

Financial Times (1997c) 'A Shift to Flexibility', 21 February.

Financial Times (1998) 'Poland Prepares for Telecoms Breakthrough', 13 January.

Flaherty, M. and Rappaport, A. (1991) *Multinational Corporations and the Environment: a Survey of Global Practices*, Center for Environmental Management, Tufts University.

Gray, C. (1996) 'In Search of Owners: Lessons of Experience with Privatization and Corporate Governance in Transition Economies', *Policy Research Working Paper*, no. 1595, Office of the Chief Economist and Senior Vice President, Development Economics, World Bank, Washington DC.

Grubb, D. and Wells, W. (1993) 'Employment Regulation and Patterns of Work in EC Countries', *OECD Economic Studies*, vol. 21, pp. 7-58.

Gual, J. and Martín, C. (1995) 'Trade and Foreign Direct Investment with Central and Eastern Europe: Its Impact on Spain' in Faini, R. and Portes, R. (eds.) *European Union Trade with Eastern Europe: Adjustment and Opportunities*, Centre for Economic Policy Research, London.

Halpern, L. (1995) 'Comparative Advantage and Likely Trade Pattern of the CEECs' in Faini, R. and Portes, R. (eds.) *European Union Trade with Eastern Europe: Adjustment and Opportunities*, Centre for Economic Policy Research, London.

Hardy, J. (1994) 'Eastern Promise? Foreign Investment in Poland', *European Business Review*, vol. 94, pp. 28-37.

The Herald (1997) 'Hyundai Incentives Called into Question', 28 November, Glasgow.

Hill, S. and Munday, M. (1995) 'Foreign Manufacturing Investment in France and the UK: a regional analysis of locational determinants', *Tijdschrift voor Economische en Sociale Geografie*, vol. 86, pp. 311-327.

HMSO (1994) *Competitiveness: Helping Business to Win*, Cm 2563, HMSO, London.

Holland, D. and Owens, J. (1995) 'Tax, Transition and Investment', *OECD Observer*, no. 193, pp. 29-31.

Houde, M.-F. (1994) 'Foreign Investment in Hungary' *OECD Observer,* no. 189, OECD, Paris, pp. 36-38.

Hughes, M. and Helinska-Hughes, E. (1997) *Greenfield Site Corporate Location in Transition Economies,* paper for the British Academy of Management annual conference, 8-10 September.

IBB (1997) *Review of Operations 1997,* Invest in Britain Bureau, London.

Industrial Development Act 1982 (various years) *Annual Report,* HMSO, London.

inforMISEP (1994) 'Fixed-Term Contracts in the European Union', *Employment Observatory: Policies,* no. 47, Employment Observatory, Commission of the European Communities, Brussels.

JETRO (1996) *The 12th Survey of European Operations of Japanese Companies in the Manufacturing Sector,* JETRO, London.

Lankes, H.-P. and Venables, T. (1996) 'Foreign Direct Investment in Economic Transition: The Changing Pattern of Investment', *The Economics of Transition,* vol. 4, pp. 331-349.

Leonard, H. (1988) *Pollution and the Struggle for the World Product: Multinational Corporations, Environment and International Advantage,* Cambridge University Press, Cambridge.

Levenstein, C. and Ellers, S. (1980) 'Are Hazardous Industries Fleeing Abroad?', *Business and Society Review,* no. 34, pp. 44-46.

LIS (1997) *Locate in Scotland: Annual Review 1996-97,* The Scottish Office Education and Industry Department, Glasgow.

Manser, R. (1993) *The Squandered Dividend - The Free Market and the Environment in Eastern Europe,* Earthscan, London.

Mella Márquez, J.-M. (1994) 'Spatial and Sectoral Strategies of Foreign Direct Investment in Spain' in Dicken, P. and Quévit, M. (eds.) *Transnational Corporations and European Regional Restructuring,* Faculty of Geographical Sciences, Utrecht University.

Mueller, F. and Purcell, J. (1992) 'The Europeanization of Manufacturing and the Decentralization of Bargaining: Multinational Management Strategies in the European Automobile Industry', *International Journal of Human Resource Management,* vol. 3, pp. 15-34.

Murdoch, A. (1997) 'Who Pays Wins', *Management Today,* April.

Neven, D. and Siotis, G. (1993) 'Foreign Direct Investment in the European Community: Some Policy Issues', *Oxford Review of Economic Policy,* vol. 9, pp. 72-93.

OECD (1991) *Taxing Profits in a Global Economy: Domestic and International Issues*, OECD, Paris.

OECD (1992) *International Direct Investment: Policies and Trends in the 1980s*, OECD, Paris.

OECD (1994) *OECD Reviews of Foreign Direct Investment: Italy*, OECD, Paris.

OECD (1995) *Taxation and Foreign Direct Investment*, OECD, Paris.

OECD (1996a) *Tax Expenditures: Recent Experiences*, OECD, Paris.

OECD (1996b) *The Environment Industry: The Washington Meeting*, OECD, Paris.

OECD (1996c) *Main Science and Technology Indicators*, no.2, OECD, Paris.

OECD (1997a) *Financial Market Trends*, 67, OECD, Paris.

OECD (1997b) *Economic Globalisation and the Environment*, OECD, Paris.

PACEC (1989) *The Efficiency of Regional Policy in Member Countries of the European Community*, P.A. Cambridge Economic Consultants, Cambridge.

PACEC (1995) *Assessment of the Wider Effects of Foreign Direct Investment in Manufacturing in the UK*, P.A. Cambridge Economic Consultants, Cambridge.

Padoa-Schioppa, T. *et al* (1987) *Efficiency, Stability and Equity: A Strategy for the Evolution of the Economic System of the European Community*, Economica, Paris.

Pain, N. and Young, G. (1996) *Tax Competition and the Pattern of European Foreign Direct Investment*, prepared for Institute for Fiscal Studies Conference on Public Policy and the Location of Economic Activity, November, London.

PAIZ (1997) *The List of Major Foreign Investors in Poland*, Warsaw.

PAIZ (1998) *Foreign Investment in Central European Countries*, Warsaw.

Raines, P. and Wishlade, F. (1997) 'Cross-European Perspectives on the Use and Control of Financial Incentives in Foreign Investment Promotion' in Danson, M., Hill, S. and Lloyd, G. (eds.) *Regional Governance and Economic Development*, Pion, London.

Recio, A. (1992) 'Economic Internationalisation and the Labour Market in Spain' in Castro, A., Méhaut, P. and Rubery, J. (eds.) *International Integration and Labour Market Organisation*, Academic Press, London.

Reid, D. (1995) *Sustainable Development: An Introduction*, Earthscan & Kogan Page, London.

Ruane, F. and Görg, H. (1997) 'The Impact of Foreign Direct Investment on Sectoral Adjustment in the Irish Economy', *National Institute Economic Review*, no. 160, pp. 76-86.

Rzeczpospolita (1997) 'Boom czeka na Prywatyzacje Monopoli', 9 September.

Rzeczpospolita (1998) 'Inwestycje: Co najmniej 150 Milionow Dolarow od Motoroli', 19 January.

Scottish Enterprise (1997) *Annual Accounts 1996-1997*, Scottish Enterprise, Glasgow.

Sheehan, M. (1993) 'Government Financial Assistance and Manufacturing Investment in Northern Ireland', *Regional Studies*, vol. 27, pp. 527-540.

Shirlow, P. (1995) 'Transnational Corporations in the Republic of Ireland and the Illusion of Economic Well-Being', *Regional Studies*, vol. 29, pp. 687-690.

Stankovsky, J. (1995) *Direct Investment in Eastern Europe*, Bank Austria, Vienna.

Stevens, C. (1992) 'The Environment Industry', *OECD Observer*, no. 177, pp. 26-28.

The Sunday Times (1997a) 'Blair to End War over Inward Investment', 28 September.

The Sunday Times (1997b) 'Regional Warfare Threatens UK plc', 12 October.

Sysdem (1995) *Employment Observatory: Trends*, no. 22, Employment Observatory, Commission of the European Communities, Brussels.

Taylor, J. (1993) 'An Analysis of the Factors Determining the Geographical Distribution of Japanese Manufacturing Investment in the UK 1984-91', *Urban Studies*, vol. 30, pp. 209-224.

Thomas, K. (1997) ''Corporate Welfare' Campaigns in North America', *New Political Economy*, vol. 2.

Thomsen, S. and Woolcock, S. (1993) *Direct Investment and European Integration - Competition among Firms and Governments*, Pinter and Royal Institute of International Affairs (RIIA), London.

The Times (1995) 'Where the Movers and Shakers End up', 18 October.

Tong, H.-M. and Walter, C. (1980) 'An Empirical Study of Plant Location Decisions of Foreign Manufacturing Investors in the United States', *Columbia Journal of World Business*, vol. 15, pp. 66-73.

Transformacja Gospodarki (1996) 'Instytut Badan nad Gospodarka Rynkowa', no. 80, pp. 1-54, Warszawa-Gdansk.

Tüselmann, H.-T. (1995) 'Standort Deutschland - is Germany losing its Appeal as an International Manufacturing Location', *European Business Review*, vol. 95, no.5, pp. 21-30.

UNCTAD (1994) *World Investment Report 1994*, United Nations Centre on Transnational Corporations, New York.

UNCTAD (1995) *World Investment Report 1995*, United Nations Conference on Trade and Development, Geneva.

UNCTAD (1996) *World Investment Report 1996*, United Nations Conference on Trade and Development, Geneva.

UNCTAD (1997) *World Investment Report 1997*, United Nations Conference on trade and Development, Geneva.

UN CTC (1985) *Environmental Aspects of the Activities of Transnational Corporations: A Survey*, United Nations Centre on Transnational Corporations, New York

UN ECE (1994) *Economic Bulletin for Europe*, vol. 46, United Nations Economic Council for Europe, New York.

UNICE (1995) *Releasing Europe's Potential through Targeted Regulatory Reform: The UNICE Regulatory Report*, Union of Industrial and Employers' Confederations of Europe, Brussels.

US Department of Commerce (1996) 'Direct Investment Positions of on a Historical-Cost Basis', *Survey of Current Business*, vol. 76, no. 7.

Vaughan, D., Scott, P. and Mickle, C. (1997) 'Environment: What Do Europe's Boardrooms Think?' in Ledgerwood, G (ed.) *Greening the Boardroom: Corporate Governance and Business Sustainability*, Greenleaf Publishing, Sheffield.

Wells, L. and Wint, G. (1990) *Marketing a Country: Promotion as a Tool for Attracting Foreign Investment*, International Finance Corporation and the Multilateral Investment Guarantee Agency, Washington DC.

Wilks, S. (1992) *Models of European Administration: DGIV and the Administration of Competition Policy*, Conference of the European Group of Public Administration, Pisa, Italy, 2-5 September.

Williams, D. (1997) 'Strategies of Multinational Enterprises and the Development of the Central and Eastern European Economies', *European Business Review,* vol. 97, pp. 134-138.

Wishlade, F. *et al* (1996) *Economic and Social Cohesion in the European Union: The Impact of Member States' Own Policies,* final report to the European Commission, European Policies Research Centre, University of Strathclyde, Glasgow.

Woolcock, S. and Thomsen, S. (1993) *Direct Investment and European Integration: Competition among Firms and Governments,* Pinter, London.

World Bank and OECD (1992) *Corporate Survey on Western Direct Investment and Environmental Issues in Central and Eastern Europe,* World Bank, New York.

World Commission on Environment and Development (1987) *Our Common Future,* Oxford University Press, Oxford.

Wyatt, D. and Dashwood, A. (1993) *European Community Law,* 3rd edition, Sweet & Maxwell, London.

Young, S. and Hood, N. (1994) 'Designing Developmental After-Care Programmes for Foreign Direct Investors in the European Union', *Transnational Corporations,* vol. 3, pp. 45-72.

Young, S., Hood, N. and Wilson, A. (1994) 'Targeting Policy as a Competitive Strategy for European Inward Investment Agencies', *European Urban and Regional Studies,* vol. 1, pp. 143-159.

Yuill, D., Allen, K., Bachtler, J., Clement, K. and Wishlade, F. (1992) *European Regional Incentives 1992-93,* 12th edition, Bowker-Saur, London.

Yuill, D., Allen, K., Bachtler, J., Clement, K. and Wishlade, F. (1993) *European Regional Incentives 1993-94,* 13th edition, Bowker-Saur, London.

Yuill, D., Allen, K., Bachtler, J., Clement, K. and Wishlade, F. (1994) *European Regional Incentives 1994-95,* 14th edition, Bowker-Saur, London.

Yuill, D., Bachtler, J. and Wishlade, F. (1996) *European Regional Incentives 1996-97,* 16th edition, Bowker-Saur, London.

Yuill, D., Bachtler, J., and Wishlade, F. (1997) *European Regional Incentives 1997-98,* 17th edition, Bowker Saur, London.

Appendix: Note on Foreign Investment Statistics

Analysis of foreign investment in Europe needs to take account of the problems of comparing FDI statistics across different countries. The comparability of FDI data is limited by the fact that countries define FDI using different operational parameters: different components of FDI - such as equity investments, reinvested earnings and intra-company loans - are treated differently by national authorities.

The problems are seen when comparing investment flows as measured by recipient countries against those from investing countries. The discrepancy in figures can very large, especially when examined through bilateral flows. For example, UK estimates of the country's investment in Germany have consistently been larger than the estimates of the German authorities, at times by almost a factor of two.

There are several limitations associated with FDI data. First, some national FDI figures focus on gross rather that net FDI flows. The former does not take into account issues such as divestment by foreign investors, which can significantly reduce the real level of FDI in any given economy. Second, some national FDI figures may reflect planned rather than actual investment, thereby inflating the true extent of some FDI projects. Third, in some countries not all foreign investments are reported to authorities by companies, so that figures may underestimate the level of new FDI. Lastly, some national FDI data, excludes mergers and acquisitions. Given the importance of this type of FDI inflow, national FDI data is often significantly lower than other, more inclusive FDI datasets.

Another problem with aggregate FDI inflow data is the lack of insight they provide into the political significance of foreign investment in any national or sub-national Western European economy. Annual FDI inflows or stocks data may conceal the true significance of foreign investment in these economies. Although annual inflows may be small by international standards, the level of FDI as a proportion of Gross Domestic Product (GDP) may be significant. Similarly, the importance of FDI in any country may vary greatly, both spatially and sectorally. In Scotland and Wales, for example, FDI is a highly sensitive issue, owing to the growing regional economic importance of foreign ownership, especially in key parts of the manufacturing sector (eg. electronics and automobiles).

In the case of Central and Eastern Europe, these problems are often more acute. Various statistical sources differ in their estimates of FDI indicators such as cumulative values, FDI inflows, and per capita amounts. All figures for FDI based on CEE sources are subject to some uncertainty, partly due to differences in the definition of FDI and varying approaches to data collection. Statistics on trans-border investment are far less reliable than those for trade, and suffer inaccuracies when applied to CEE despite adoption of IMF guidelines (see Stankovsky, 1995). The fact that various institutions compile FDI data complicates matters further. Although Poland defines FDI in accordance with the OECD definition, there are three sources of data on FDI in Poland (the Polish Agency for Foreign Investment, Central Office of Statistics and National Bank of Poland) (*Rzeczpospolita*,1997).

An important feature of this issue is the trigger point at which data are recorded. This varies from complete inclusion where FDI inflows are relatively small and there is reasonable consensus on values (eg. Slovakia), to cases where there is an alarming degree of inconsistency. A good example would be Poland where amounts less than US$ 1 million are not included in official databases and observers often chose to include their own estimates of this unrecorded volume (*Rzeczpospolita*, 1997). Consequently, figures for both FDI stock and year-on-year flows, based on our comparisons, can vary by as much as 15-20 percent.

Even data for the same country between years can be subject to serious distortion due to a small number of large investment projects, or even a single, large acquisition or greenfield site development. Therefore, the area of quantification of national, regional and sectoral distribution of FDI is problematic. In addition, more detailed analyses which might relate specific FDI projects to the effectiveness of attraction measures or particular forms of investment mode remains difficult other than at more local or corporate levels. Hence the reliance upon survey and case study methodology for this type of data (Lankes and Venables, 1996; Estrin and Richet, 1996).